RAINBOWS ACROSS THE OUTBACK

AN OUTBACK AUSTRALIAN ANTHOLOGY

GWENNETH LEANE

PUBLISHER
Kylie Margaret Leane
kmlpublishing.com

COVER ART/DESIGN/ILLUSTRATIONS
Kylie Leane

© 2021 Gwenneth Leane
All rights reserved.

No portion of this publication may be reproduced or transmitted, in any form or by any means, without the prior written permission of either copyright owner or publisher of this book.

RAINBOWS ACROSS THE OUTBACK
An Outback Australian Anthology
PUBLICATION HISTORY

Paperback Edition / June 2021 Gwenneth Leane
ISBN: 978-0-6451032-1-2

PRINTED IN AUSTRALIA

For information address:
gwen.leane@gmail.com
authorkylieleane@gmail.com

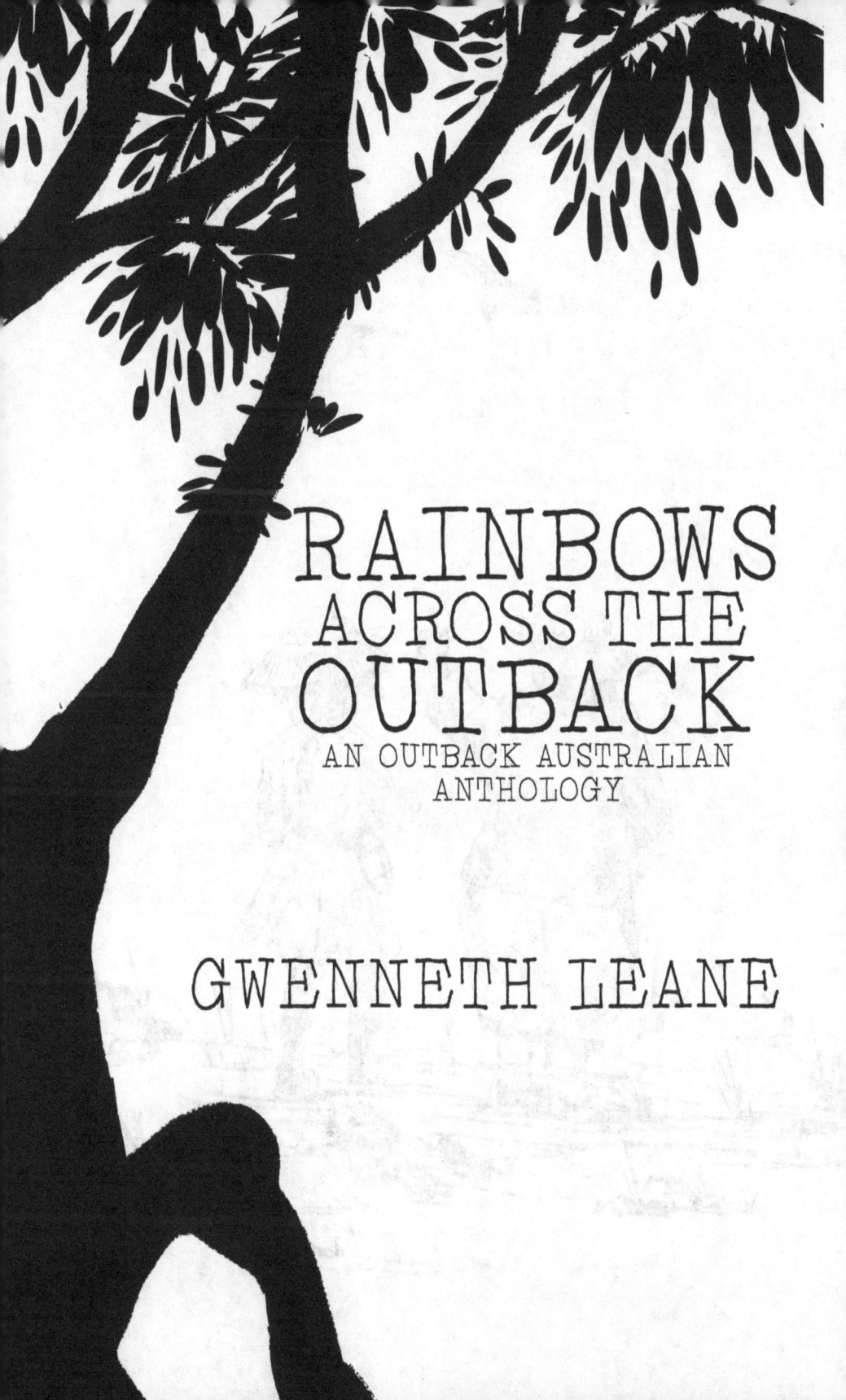

RAINBOWS ACROSS THE OUTBACK

AN OUTBACK AUSTRALIAN ANTHOLOGY

GWENNETH LEANE

THE SHORT CUT

Molly Walsh and Lilly Costello left mid-morning, heading for Marla Bore. They were travelling along the Oodnadatta Track in a Toyota four-wheel drive Land Cruiser belonging to the South Australian Housing Trust for whom they both worked.

'Something dead out there, Molly, eagles circling.' Lilly pointed skyward to her left. Her eyes mere slits against the glare as she took in the sights and smells along the trail the old people had walked through the ages.

'Yes. Let's hope it's an animal and not someone lost.' Molly murmured.

'I remember my grandfather telling me never to follow a willywag tail. He will lead you to someone. He's a messenger.' She had noticed the erratic flight of the excitable little black and white bird between bushes.

The wind cooled her face through the open window. The scent of the bush filled her nostrils and heightened her perception of the presence of the old ones. Were they trying to tell her something, she mused.

The brown ribbon of road along which they sped, wound through weirdly eroded flat-topped hills of brilliant red, yellow and white sandstone. These hills marked the personal Dreaming of many of the old ones, and were known by the whites as the Painted Hills

Both women were the offspring of white fathers and Aboriginal mothers. Both had spent their childhood with the Family before being taken into a children's Home to be civilised.

In later years when they returned, they found they were aliens among their people because they didn't know the language or the culture. Civilization hadn't given them the right of passage in the white Family either.

Mid morning they pulled up in a patch of scrub growing between high red sand-hills.

'There was a big fight here.' Lilly recalled the story told many times around campfires of her childhood. A brooding deathly silence lay over the scrub. The women felt it.

' Yes, lots of spirits here.' Molly agreed shivering. She didn't believe in the Dream - time, having been Christianised. But she sensed the power of the Dreaming.

'Men from a family in Western Australia came across the desert and tried to steal our women.' Lilly even thought she could hear the clash of spears and cries of the dying. 'They went away without the women and a few less of their own.' There was a note of familial pride in her voice.

'If the raiders had been successful, we might have been Western Australians.'

Both women chuckled.

Molly driving, they jouncing over the rutted road that hadn't seen a grader for months, their progress pinpointed by a dust plume

'We used to travelled everywhere by camel. I had my own camel.' Molly recalled. 'My father made a box and harnessed it to the camel. I used to sit in it and go to sleep.' Molly's face was soft at the thought of her father. 'Dad was a good man. He kept us well clothed and fed. When he died that's when I had to go into the Children's Home.'

' I don't remember my father.' Lilly sighed, 'He was always away. My mother couldn't look after five of us and the Police came and took us to the Home.'

The women searched the past for rare gems of memories. Trying to rediscover what had been taken from them.

'We'd better find a place to camp, Lilly?' They were now travelling across undulating plains. Long shadows stretched across the landscape. The mystery of night was beginning to fill the gullies and washes.

'Yes, the sun's getting low,' Lilly agreed

'Those trees over there would make a good camp,' Molly pointed to the right.

'I don't feel good about camping here, it's as if something is wrong. Let's go a bit further.' Lilly continued driving into the westering sun.

'Hey! look over there in those trees. A car!' Molly pointed to the right.

'What's a car doing out here? Maybe it broke down.'

'Better stop and see if they need help.'

Both women sat in their vehicle for long minutes before leaving it wondering if a trap had been set.

'Wonder if anyone is around?'

'Don't see anyone?'

The women got out of their Cruiser, and stood close the vehicle in case danger lurked.

'Halloo, anyone there?' Lilly's call echoed across the desert.

'No one seems to be around.' Molly agreed. 'The car isn't stuck.'

'Wonder who it is? The car is not familiar?'

'It doesn't belong to any of ours.'

Lilly laughed, 'No, it's in too good a condition.' Molly began to circle around, looking for tracks. She called, 'Over here, there are two sets of tracks. They went this way.'

'Maybe they ran out of water and went to look for some.' Worry lines creased the women's' faces. 'The eagles - could that have been these people?' Lilly hardly dared to express her thoughts.

'No,' Molly asserted. 'That was miles back.'

'Molly, people walk miles when lost. I didn't see any containers in the car, did you.'

'It looks like they sat down here? Wonder if they were hurt or something.'

'Welbourne Hill Station is the closest place, but it's still a long way off and in the wrong direction.' Lilly looked across the rolling plains of red gibbers and stunted blue bush, trying to catch a movement.

'It'll be dark soon. We should see if we can find them.' Molly looked around then returned to where it seemed the strangers had sat.

'Their tracks lead back toward the painted hills. Why didn't they follow the road?'

Worry lines deepened the brackets at the corners of their mouths, their hearts cold. The tracks led backwards to where they'd seen the eagles.

Molly pointed to the east, 'Over that way, they're over that way.'

The two women returned to the car, retracing their earlier journey. With unerring sense of direction they drew up at the place where earlier they had noticed the eagles. They set off carrying a flask of water each and big torches, their stock in trade when in the bush. The spot where the eagles circled had unconsciously been noted, now even though dusk was closing in they were able to find the low mulga clad rise.

'Around here somewhere,' Molly muttered.

'Just hope we're not too late, Lilly. We don't know how long they've been out here.'

'Coo-eee,' Molly yelled

There was a faint cry not far to the right. The women stumbled across Spinifex, stones, stunted salt - bush in their haste.

'Are you all right?' Molly and Lilly knelt beside a young man and girl, putting the bottles to their lips, dripping water over their mouths

'Thank God!' the young man breathed, and reached for the bottle but Lilly held it away from him.

'Jenny, is she all right? She just gave up and lay down,' the boy croaked.

'No, Jenny's in a bad way. We must get help for her.' Molly stood up. There was a question on Lilly's face as she looked up, Molly's brown eyes held the answer.

'What are you doing roaming around out here in this country with out water?' Lilly wanted to know.

'We stopped to have lunch. We took our sandwiches and went and sat down over behind a sand hill. The view was lovely. We thought we knew the way back.' He sounded like a croaking frog. The boy had taken off his shirt and was as red and blistered as a fried tomato, his lips dry and swollen.

Lilly half carried the boy back to the car.

'I've got to go back and help Molly with Jenny.'

'Is Jenny all right?' The boy recovering insisted.

'Yes! But she is unconscious.' her heart was crying as she admitted, 'I hope we aren't too late.'

'Please help her.' The boy whispered weakly.

Lilly returned to help Molly.

Night had fallen as they placed Jenny beside the boy on the back seat of the Land cruiser.

He took her limp hand in his, tears flooding down his cheeks.

'It was our honey moon.' he sobbed. 'Thank you for looking for us, we wont forget what you have done.'

The women smiled at each other. It had been reaffirmed to them that they were the children of the land and belonged to the Family. Civilisation had taken them away and tried to graft them into another family, and though they had adopted other beliefs the old ones hadn't deserted them.

How did you know where to find us?' The boy's voice was strengthening.

'We saw the eagles circling and a willywag tail.' Lilly spoke softly wondering how her words would be received, 'seeing those birds gave us a strong feeling that something was wrong. Then we found your empty car and began to search for tracks.'

The engine roared into life, Molly turned the car and they sped back towards Oodnadatta and help.

THE CITY SLICKER

Into the bush the City Slicker drove
'I need a change of scene,' he sighed
He pulled the van beneath a grand old gum
The scrolls of bark he didn't see
The smooth white tree trunk was ignored.
Ants racing to and fro went unnoticed
'Why doesn't someone clean up all this bark,' he griped.

The City Slicker slept beneath his doona
So he never saw the black lace trees
Outlined against a whitening dawn.
He didn't see the mountain crags
Kissed orange red by a rising sun.
Nor did he hear the wild orchestra
Of parrot, kookaburra, crow.
He woke just in time for brunch

'Where's the aero guard?' The City Slicker yelled
As he waved 'Good Day' to the flies
The bearded dragon, statue still, watched every move
The eagle floating in the sky went unseen
Rosellas flashed like jewels through the bush
As he washed down eggs and bacon with a beer

GWENNETH LEANE

'What's out here to see?' the City Slicker wondered
As he switched the telly to Australian Rules
'The bush is empty. There's nothing to do.'
The flash of butterflies was ignored as they
Tasted nectar from the blossom cups
But then, he never saw the creamy blossoms either
The TV had hypnotised him with its charms

'Let's have a BBQ' he smiled
The aroma of fried sausage, steak and onions
Wafted through the bush
The cicadas loudly strummed but the sausages were louder still
The red and orange drama of a setting sun was ignored
As was the dingo's lonely howl and hoot of owl
'It's this country air,' he sighed and closed his eyes.

The City slicker boasted loud
'I've been to the bush. There's nothing but trees.
It's boring I'll never go again.'
'Roos sat up tall and wondered at the roar
With broomsticks for legs and dusters for feathers
The emus joined his race to town.
He never knew he'd been surrounded
By the many creatures great and small.

RAINBOWS ACROSS THE OUTBACK

GWENNETH LEANE

THE EMU

Strutting across the saltbush plain
With lordly grace on legs like stalks
The emu searched for a meal of seeds
His drumming call danced from dune to dune
His feathers flounced in the wind
As a mop; wings deformed
A brain the size of a blip
He's grounded on earth forever.

THE ORPHAN

Dog-Fence Story

The match flared into life. Jacki McIntosh pushed it into a pile of leaves and twigs. Blue smoke lazily drifted upwards; she coughed.

'Come on, burn,' she cursed, leaning down, blowing into the smoking debris. She coughed again to clear her lungs of the acrid smoke. A flame licked up through the sticks into a blaze; she piled on more wood to feed the hungry flames.

Jacki stood, her breath caught in awe, as the last rays of the sun turned the salt lake into a sheet of orange fire.

'Come on, girl. Don't stand there dreamin',' the old man growled. 'It'll be dark soon. We gotta get the camp set up before dark.'

'OK, Dad,' Jacki turned to the Toyota truck and hoisted out their swags. Next came the folding table and chairs and finally the icebox with the foodstuffs. She glanced toward the Lake; the brilliance was dying just like her hopes of getting a life for herself. She glanced behind at the dunes. They, too, were fiery red-lit by the sun's dying rays. A lone dingo stood sentinel on top of the highest dune. His yellow coat burnished gold. Jacki marvelled at the magnificent creature, its head raised proudly as its nose studied the air.

'Stop being a tragedy queen, girl,' the old man grumbled. 'I gotta mend the fence before that dingo gets through. Heaven knows how many others have gone through. Get the damper made and the stew heating while I check the fence for holes up ahead. I should shoot the bugger to make sure he doesn't get through the fence.'

'Yes, Dad!' Jacki sighed. It was easier to comply than to fight his authority. For as long as she could remember, she had lived with the older man. He was a boundary rider along the dog fence that ran five thousand kilometres across Australia, providing a barrier between the dingo and the flocks and herds of landholders in four states. According to the older man, as she thought of him, her father had given her to him to look after until he returned from sheep shearing in Queensland. But her father had never returned—extensive enquiries as to where her father had disappeared met a wall of silence. The older man took over her care.

She supposed she should be grateful to him for giving her food and clothing, even if it was boys' clothing. She had never worn a dress in her life. Everyone thought she was a boy. The older man said it was safer that way, and she had accepted what he said.

The Lake was no longer on fire but a dull grey. Like my life, she thought. If only – for what did she long? The emptiness of her life stretched before her. The School of the Air teachers urged the older man to let her go to University and study, but he refused on the pretext her father might turn up looking for her.

The fire had died into a pile of fiery coals. The damper in the camp oven was buried in the coals and would be cooked by now. The stew was simmering on a grid over the embers. The evening hush was broken by the howl of dingoes in the dunes, sending shivers up her spine. The girl lit the pressure lantern, and a pool of yellow light ballooned around her, making the night even darker.

Where was the older man? He should have been back by now. She stirred the stew and took the damper from the coals. The odour of baked damper filled the night air, and Jacki felt ravenous. Breaking off a piece, she dipped it in the stew and ate the morsel. It was delicious; she wanted more but decided to wait until the older man returned.

Unease filled Jacki over the failure of his return. She climbed the nearest dune to see if headlights were flashing, but the night was dark and silent. Back at the camp, she built the camp-fire into a massive blaze so the older man could find his way if the vehicle had broken down and he was on foot. Time passed slowly, and still, he hadn't returned. Taking up the lantern and a gun, her heart racing, Jacki set out on foot along the fence-line in search of the older man. Where was he? What had happened to him? Had he ran off and left her? Jacki began to wonder what she would do without him. She realized he'd been a buffer between her and loneliness. She'd been wrong to want to get away from him; he was her safety net.

Jacki called out; her voice echoed across the desert. A dingo howled close by, and she put the lantern down and fired at two eyes. The shot filled the night and then became lost in the vast silence. Picking up the light, she started to run, calling the older man's name.

Was that a voice up ahead? To get an idea of where she was, Jacki tried to remember what the land looked like in daylight. She called again. Yes, that was a voice. It was weak and held fear. Hurrying as fast as she dared, Jacki came up to the Toyota. Looking about, she saw the hole in the fence patched. Where the older man had walked along the fence line, but where was he?

'Dad? Where are you,' Jacki hadn't called him Dad in ages.

'Here, girl, quick! I'm finished.'

Jacki lifted the light in the voice's direction; the older man supported himself on a nearby bush. The older man had unsuspectingly fallen into a morass of slime left by a flood during the last storm. Horror gripped Jacki, and she just stood frozen. Mud was seeping into the old man's mouth as his lips formed 'Help.'

Fear galvanized Jacki into action. She turned the Toyota around to give more light, grabbed a rope from the back of the truck, and coiled it into a noose. Jacki cast it at the older man's head, tightening it as much as she dared without choking him, hoping to keep his head up. Then searching the shadows for logs, she carried several fallen trees and laid them over the mud. With the help of the rope tied to the truck, she edged along the branches towards the older man, hoping to get the line around his shoulders to be able to pull him out. He was very still and hadn't spoken. Eventually, she reached him. Scrabbling through the mud, she wiggled the rope over his shoulders, securing it so it wouldn't slip off and choke him. She slithered back to the Toyota and started the motor, reversing it slowly, hoping to be able to drag her surrogate parent out. Gradually the mud gave up its trophy, and the old one lay on the solid ground. He was still.

She became aware of being surrounded by several sets of eyes shining on the edge of the light. 'You bloody killers,' she shouted, picked up the gun, and fired at the nearest pair. There was a scream. Quickly the eyes vanished, and a body thrashed in the bushes in its death throes.

'Got ya,' she muttered. She couldn't stop to think about being afraid; she had to save the man who saved her. She owed him big time. With the last of her water, she washed his face; it was deathly pale. She cleaned inside his mouth and dribbled in water. The man gave a feeble swallow. Encouraged, Jacki dribbled in more water. With a large swallow, he opened his eyes and looked at her. She put her arms around the filthy form and hugged him. Tears of thankfulness fell on the mud-caked face.

'Come on; we've got to get you into the truck and find help for you.'

'I'm OK.'

'No, you're not!'

In the east, the sky was whitening; soon, it would be dawn. Jacki pulled the older man to the truck. How was she going to get him into the vehicle?

From out of the gloom, another Toyota appeared. 'What's happened here?' Jacki recognized him as the young roo shooter, Snow Costello. He stared in disbelief at the mud-caked man and bedraggled girl.

A girl! What's she doing out here? He registered. He had not realized the old fencer's off-sider was a girl. He was speechless. How had the old boundary-rider kept the girl's identity a secret for so long? Her name – of course – Jacki, it could be a girl or boy. Under all that mud was a pretty young woman.

'What's happened?' Alarm threaded through his voice as he took in the situation anew.

'Dad was fixing the fence when he slipped and fell into the patch of quicksand in the wash away.'

'I'll call the Flying Doctor on wireless radio to meet us at the homestead.' Snow took control as he climbed from the vehicle. Together, he and the girl hefted the older man into the passenger seat of their Toyota.

'Are you up to driving to the homestead? It's only a couple of miles away. I'll follow it. Gotta get my quota of kangaroo carcasses into the chiller at the homestead before they go rotten,' Snow explained. Trying to cover his surprise at Jacki, suddenly turning into a woman.

'I can drive,' Jacki defended, annoyed at Snow talking down to her. 'Do you think Dad will be all right?' she added in a subdued voice.

'You bet. Your Dad's a tough old geezer. The Doc will fix him up,' Snow looked at the girl again,

' So, you are a girl?'

The roo shooter was still bemused by Jacki being a girl.

'Dad didn't want anyone to know I was a girl because he thought I wouldn't be safe out here among most men, and he wouldn't send me away.'

'What was he going to do when you grew up?'

'I dunno. I want to go away and get a job somewhere. I hate it out here.'

Just as they took off towards the homestead, the sun broke across the dunes. As they drove around the Lake again, the salt-encrusted surface turned into apricot brilliance at the dawn of a new day.

If Jacki had had the second sight, she'd have known it was the beginning of a new life.

RAINBOWS ACROSS THE OUTBACK

WINDING RIVER STATION

A Drabble

Jack sat astride his red horse on a rocky outcrop surveying Winding Rivers Station. It was a quarter the size of Tasmania.
'It's been a good year, Jill,' Jack smiled his satisfaction. 'You'd better start planning an itinerary for next year.'
Jill's eyes were on the homestead, 'Jack, the house is on fire.'
'Bloody Hell,' Jack exclaimed, spurring his horse into an instant gallop. Jill followed.
The couple slid to a stop amid dust and smoke. Water was gushing into the heart of the flames from the Station fire truck. Curly Winston was on the grader removing litter and debris away from the house to save the sheds and cattle yards. The horses had been set free.
'Jack, come back,' Jill screamed.
'I've got to get the hard drive,' Jack's reply was muffled in the roar of flames.
Jack tied a hanky over his mouth and stumbled to the safe in the wall. His fingers stung from the hot safe; he fumbled the combination. The safe opened, and Jack grabbed the little box, just as he turned to leave an inner wall caved in, clothes alight Jack raced for the door.
'All our business is on that hard drive; I had to save it.' Jack collapsed at Jill's feet.
The station foreman and a jackaroo threw blankets over Jack to put out the flames and carried him to the sickbay.
Jack's burns proved superficial, and after being dressed, Jack could walk outside to view the blackened skeleton that was the homestead.
'This is the last straw, Jill, the bank will not stand us finance anymore.'
Jill laughed, 'Jack, I haven't been able to tell you, but my mother has passed away yesterday and left me her estate. What's this about finished? We've only just begun. Winding Rivers will be debt-free; the overseas trip is safe.'

THE HYDROLOGIST

We found him sitting in an experimental shaft dug into the wall of an abandoned opal mine. It was just above the water level of a cutting that flooded when the miner excavated for opal. The hydrologist was reading the paper; several books lay strewn beside him.

Above the cut, the opal field shimmered under fifty-degree heat. I was gasping, longing for a cool place. We heard about a flooded mineshaft used as a swimming pool and went in search. We found not only the water-filled cutting but also a man who had seen the ideal spot to while away a few hours on a Sunday.

We swam and played in the water, mentally thanking the miner who excavated the mine only to lose it to the rising water table. We speculated about the fortune he might have missed.

The hydrologist was a quiet man; his greeting lacked enthusiasm. My husband, Bruce, is a hail-fellow-well-met kind of person. Eventually, the hydrologist thawed and related his story to us briefly. He had begun life in Europe studying hydrology and gaining a degree. He decided to immigrate to Australia, hoping for a better experience, settling in the north of Western Australia.

Poor English made him a laughing stock among his Aussie workmates. He became more isolated and hurt and withdrew from society. Nursing his hurts, he arrived on the opal field, mining for opal.

He became the swimming pool's unofficial keeper, cleaning up the used nappies, empty hair shampoo bottles, and other debris left by careless users of the swimming pool. The area degraded with rubbish made one feel sick at the sight and not want to swim. When the place became too bad, the hydrologist would set off some dynamite and blow the pool out. It would be clean again for a while.

The hydrologist found many nationalities on the opal field. He no longer stood out as a freak. He found a niche where he was accepted. He was able to be himself, and so he quietly settled into the community. Many ethnic groups seeking a different lifestyle made up the community;

he was considered just another fortune seeker. He gave up working as a hydrologist to feel safe.

The collection of sheds, caravans, and shacks could hardly be called a town. The people living there came from every part of the globe. Bruce felt privileged to hear the hydrologist's story.

We were misfits ourselves, arriving on the field to mine not knowing a soul and even less about mining. We were the laughing stock of the community. We were misfits because our three co-miners were Aboriginals. Racism on the field was alive, and well, we became the butt of many jokes.

As for us, being shunned was no big deal; we would only be there a short time, then we would leave. Like many others of our ilk, we were searching for a fortune, so being a misfit was a small price to pay.

BIRTHSTONE

'I feel lucky, Sam. I've got a good feeling; I'm sure we'll find some opal.' Gillian Winters could hardly contain her excitement as they bounced over the dusty, rutted track between mountains of white dirt in the Falcon station wagon.

'Dunno why we had to travel into the outback to find your birthstone. You could've bought an opal ring in the city cheaper and with much less fuss.' Sam's jowls shook with exasperation. His physical attributes were far from perfect, and his shortness and width made him resemble a barrel.

'My horoscope predicted I'd find riches, adventure and romance this week. It's been one of my ambitions to go opal mining,' Gillian said.

'Harrumph! Since when!' Sam said cynically. 'This place looks like it's got the chickenpox with all these white mounds and holes in the ground.'

'Oh, these hills are called mullock heaps. I read about it in the Gem Finders mag.'

'What! So, you don't read your horoscope anymore?'

Gillian ignored his needling. After all, she'd been putting up with it for ten years. She often wondered why she didn't leave. It was like being married to a little boy inside a man's body. He was good at playing the blame game, leaving her feeling like a worm of the lowest order.

Sam allowed the station wagon to roll to a stop on the edge of the mining area. The view before them was not what they expected of an opal field. It was more like a moonscape. After the teeming crowds of Adelaide, the vast nothingness stunned them for a moment, and their bickering ceased.

'Well, where do we start digging?' Gillian undid her seatbelt and opened the door, trying to buoy her flagging spirits.

'How do I know? I'm only the slave around here.' Sam had never had any vision for the project. He was the proverbial couch potato and wanted to spend the holidays watching the Easter races on SKY Channel. Gillian nagged him so that Sam consented to travel to Coober Pedy in the remote north of South Australia in search of opal for the sake of peace.

'Let's find a pub. It will at least have cold beer,' Sam grumbled.

'Damn your beer. That's all you think about – booze.' Disgusted, Gillian looked at Sam with a critical eye as she climbed from the wagon, wondering what it would take to make Sam take an interest in himself. He had put on weight these last years. She was always telling him to lay off the beer and exercise more.

'A man has to have some pleasures in life. Besides, it helps dull the pain of roaming all over the bloody country with a nagging wife.' His frustration put an edge of cruelty in his reply.

Gillian lifted her chin, the only sign that his words had wounded, and walked ahead of him. Their arguments always ended in this fashion, trading insults and Gillian walking off in a huff.

He knew he'd said too much. Well, perhaps he had, but he was already sick of the flies, the heat, and the dust, and they'd only been in the place half a day, and they had the whole weekend to go. Inwardly he groaned; how could he persuade Gilly to forget the damned opal-mining thing and go home? Well, he'd better offer an olive branch to make the next few days bearable. 'From what I see of it, you just dig where it suits you.'

'Come on, then,' Gillian accepted the olive branch, trudging up a small rise to get a better view of the surrounding desert. 'Down there to the right of the station wagon looks a good place to start. Unload the tools.'

Sam put the picks and shovels in the wheelbarrow and followed her. Gillian's natural optimism rose as she grabbed the pickaxe and brought it down with a resounding thud. The metal rang on stony ground, a feather of dust curled away.

Gillian picked at the hard-stony earth while Sam shovelled the loosened dirt into the barrow and dumped it a few yards away. They worked under the broiling sun until, in frustration and exhaustion, Gillian groaned and placed her hand on her aching back. 'It's so hard. I had no idea it would be like this.' She threw the pick down, never wanting to see it again, looking at her hands. They were blistered, raw and already painful. She tried to wipe them clean on her shorts.

'Gilly, we've been out here for two bloody hours and got nowhere. It's as hot as hell,' complained Sam. 'Let's go back to the hotel.'

'It certainly isn't any good going on like this.' Gillian pushed back tendrils of sweat-damp hair and climbed out of the shallow trough, disgruntled at having to concede defeat.

Her brief white shorts were grey. Her long graceful legs and arms had taken on the colour of boiled lobsters from the sun's rays.

Sam's usually dark jowls were like ripe tomatoes. White salt rings edged the sweat stains under his arms and down the back of his navy singlet. His shorts were strung on his buttocks, threatening to drop at any moment. He stood knee-deep in the shallow trench they'd managed to carve out of the hard earth.

'Doesn't look like any opal here; I told you it was a silly idea,' he grumbled.

'Sam, there has to be a better way.' Gillian could see her dream of finding her birthstone turning to dust. What seemed natural back in the city suddenly became impossible here under the blazing sun amid white, glaring, mullock heaps. She could see that Sam would never let her forget this. But how to gracefully admit defeat?

'I'm not staying out here another minute. I need a cold beer.'

'You don't need a beer. You look six months pregnant as it is.' Gillian scoffed. Then a sudden idea hit her. 'OK. We'll go back to the town and ask someone. They're bound to know where we can dig for opal.' She jumped behind the steering wheel, turning on the ignition as Sam flopped into the passenger's seat, in danger of being left behind as renewed enthusiasm fired Gillian's tired body.

Neither spoke as they dodged mineshafts, mullock heaps and potholes on their way into Coober Pedy. A pall of dust lay over the collection of caravans, tin sheds and doors leading to homes dug into hillsides.

'Is this Coober Pedy?' Gillian questioned doubtfully, 'There are so many roads. Where do they all go? Everything is so dusty. How can anyone live here? What a terrible place. There isn't even a tree in sight,' disappointment overwhelmed her again.

'I don't see anything that even looks like a pub,' said Sam, his head swivelling as he looked left and right. By the side of the road, a car door leant drunkenly against a post bearing the painted words "Desert Hotel, Cool Beer, half a kilometre."

'There's the pub. Gill. Pullover,' Sam was thrilled.

'Call that a pub?' Gillian observed, taking in the roughly built shop-front of dirty glass double doors flanked on either side with recycled windows. The frontage appeared constructed against the side of a hill. It was late in the day, and a few old battered vehicles were parked outside.

Sam wasted no time with gentlemanly manners. He leapt from the wagon and quickly disappeared through the double doors, leaving Gillian to make her way. Sam was already seated at a table when she entered.

'I've ordered a jug of beer and some orange juice for you,' Sam said, licking his thick lips in anticipation.

Gillian sat down and looked around, shocked. There was a line of dust-streaked men standing at the bar; two tired-looking women sat at a corner table. Didn't anyone clean the place? The room smelt of hops, cigarette smoke and stale sweat, but it was blessedly cool.

Sam was on his third glass of beer when the tall, well-built figure of a man joined them.

'G' day!'

Sam and Gillian looked up into a pair of glittering brown eyes.

'G' day!' They chorused. Gillian shivered. Is he a heart-stopper, or is he not? She suddenly became interested in her orange drink. Then on a sudden thought, I must look a complete wreck. I knew I should've cleaned up before we came in here. The wind had whipped her hair into rats' tails, and she patted at it futilely.

'Sit down,' Sam invited expansively, the alcohol beginning to take effect, as he pushed a chair out from the table with his foot. 'Have a beer on me. I'm Sam Winters. Here is my wife, Gillian.' He extended a gnarled, dirty hand the size of a shovel towards the stranger.

The newcomer ignored the proffered chair and pulled out the one beside Gillian, and sat down. 'I'm Mario Pappas, an opal miner. How far have you two come today?' he probed.

'We're from Adelaide,' Gillian explained, her breath catching in her throat. What's happening to me? She wondered. I'm behaving like a teenager, instead of a long - time married woman.

In a grubby shirt and jeans, a waiter slopped the second jug of beer and a glass of orange juice in front of them. Sam downed the contents without stopping to take a breath.

'Cheers!' Mario responded, lifting his glass and taking a sip, 'Thinking of doing some mining?'

'Yep! My wife's mad about opals being her birthstone. She wanted to use the Easter break to see if we could dig up some. Know any good spots?'

'Well, I might. Have you got a licence?' Mario asked.

'What!' they chorused.

'You have to have a licence and peg a claim,' Mario informed them. 'You are not allowed to mine anywhere. You might be on another's property and get yourself killed.' Mario cautioned them.

'We didn't know about getting licences,' Gillian admitted guiltily.

'I own a mine.' Mario's voice dropped away so that Sam had to lean forward to hear; a smile touched his lips; this was too easy, he thought. I didn't know there were any such innocents left in the world. He was thinking of a fatter bank balance as he bled them dry. Summing up Sam and Gillian, he guessed she was starved for attention and would provide him with other enjoyments in the bedroom before he got rid of them. Gillian was beautiful.

Gillian blushed under Mario's scrutiny. And hoped Sam hadn't noticed her confusion. Glancing at Sam to see if he noticed, but busy emptying the jug into his glass.

'Seeing as you don't have a licence and won't be able to get one until after the long weekend, why don't you come in as a partner with me and help finance the dig?' Mario suggested to Sam.

'Done!' Sam proffered his large hand, and Mario grasped it briefly.

'But Sam! Wait. What kind of finance is involved in the partnership?' Gillian cautioned, trying to catch Sam's eye. But he refused to look at her. If she wanted to go mining, here was an opportunity, so blast her; she'd better mine.

'No buts Gill, Mario has kindly offered a great deal. It'd be pretty poor of us if we refused now.'

'Gilly's right.' interrupted Mario. 'I need to explain that if you two come in as my partners, it means that when we find opal, you'll get 10 per cent of the profit. Because I'll supply all the equipment and cover costs, I'll take the more significant share.'

'There you go, Gill. I know a good deal when I hear one,' Sam crowed.

Despite Mario's plausible explanation, Gillian felt apprehensive about the offer. She needed to get Sam alone and talk to him. But when he locked onto an idea, there was no persuading him otherwise. Besides, he was beginning to show the effects of too much heat and too much cold beer.

'We need to talk, Sam,' she said firmly. 'I think we should find somewhere clean to stay.'

'The Star Hotel is nice and clean. Excellent service and food,' Mario said, his eyes glittered, full of promises as he held Gillian's gaze. *Ooh, he was a spine-tingling Romeo. It's years since another man has looked at me as an attractive woman.* Gillian almost drooled; the experience was so enjoyable. *Besides, he knows how to charm a woman. Not like bumbling old Sam. He wouldn't leave me in a strange place at the mercy of some Lothario while he got drunk. Could Mario be the romantic element my horoscope predicted?* Gillian sighed, peeping at Mario from the corner of her eyes. *Oh, he was such a good-looking man that she doubted her instincts.*

'Let's have another drink for the road,' Sam urged Mario.

'Lay off, Sam. You've had enough. Let's go and find the Star Hotel and book in. I could use a shower and something to eat; then we can talk business.' Her pleas fell on deaf ears.

'Don't tell me what to do, woman,' Sam was becoming belligerent and called for another jug.

Mario drained his glass, replacing it on the table, 'No thanks, Sam. I've had enough for now.' He rose from the table with animal grace; moving to Gillian's side, he bent over her possessively. She could smell his after-shave, and her fingers itched with the desire to trail her fingers through his curling hair and down his smooth-shaven cheek. *I've never looked at* another man, she thought, I'm a married woman. I do take my marriage vows seriously. But ooh, Mario is so attractive. I've always followed my star sign, and it's never let me down yet, except when I married Sam. Back then, he was handsome and robust. What happened between our honeymoon and now, she wondered, thinking back over the years? There were no children, and they had just drifted into a relationship that fitted like an old shoe. Gillian wondered why she hadn't done a course of some sort, taken up charity work or got a job. She was just as much to blame as Sam.

'Why not stay with me. I have an empty house.' Mario whispered into her ear, startling Gillian out of her reverie. It was as if he read her thoughts.

'No!' Panic forced the word from her lips. A picture of what might happen between her and Mario flashed across her mind. Have I the will power to resist him? Do I want to?

'Sam's very independent. He'll want to go to the hotel,' she hedged, her senses were reeling at the proximity of this handsome man who was wooing her – yes, wooing her.

'How about I ring the Star and find out if there are any vacancies?' Mario breathed in her ear.

Bemused, she uttered, 'OK. That's probably a good idea.'

In a few minutes, Mario was back, 'There aren't any vacancies, so come to my home.'

'But there must be other hotels around?' Gillian was desperate to keep control. Mario was forcing things along too quickly. Caution told Gillian not to trust this man; even though he was charming, he had an ulterior motive, and it wasn't helping them to mine for opal.

'No! I'm afraid there aren't any other places. Coober Pedy isn't a huge place, you know.'

Gillian was in a corner; she glanced at Sam; there was no help from that quarter. He was busy draining the jug of its contents. Before she could decide, Mario took control.

'Don't worry about Sam,' he urged, flashing white even teeth. 'He can follow along. Come on, you drive, and I'll navigate.'

It was nice having someone make decisions for her, she had to admit.

Sam couldn't organise himself out of a paper bag. That was another thing wrong with their relationship. Over the years, Sam had left her to make the decisions.

'Whatever I say, you override anyway. So, you may as well do what you want.' Sam complained. Doubts began to insert themselves into Gillian's thoughts; had she been guilty, as Sam pointed out?

Mario's hand was firm on her elbow as she stood up, her senses were on fire, yet she hesitated. This too handsome man left no doubt in her mind that he was targeting her.

'But what about Sam? I've never left him in this state before?' She hesitated, looking over her shoulder at her husband. His head was now resting on the table.

'Don't worry about Sam.' Mario dismissed him as he would some microbe. 'I'll come back for him later. I'll take you home first so you can clean up,' Mario invited.

'What about your wife? Won't she object to having strangers in her home without notice?'

'My wife is away visiting her mother.' Mario replied, his eyes glittering with desire.

That little fear raised its head; something is very, very wrong, Gillian thought in rising panic.

'Hey! Where are you'se two going,' Sam yelled unexpectedly, 'Wait for me.' He lurched to his feet. 'Don't think you can run out on me and take all the opals.' The chair crashed to the floor, and beer glasses rolled off and smashed as Sam sagged under the wobbling table.

'Oh, Sam.' Gillian cried out in concern as she raced back to him. She tugged at his prone body, trying to set him up, knowing the habit of years would not allow her to walk out and leave him.

Mario pushed her aside and roughly hauled Sam to his feet, 'C'mon, you old soak.' To Gillian's amazement, he hefted Sam over his shoulder like a sack of potatoes, carrying him to their station wagon. Sam was dumped on the back seat.

Mario's arm stretched across the back of the seat just above her shoulders. He directed her through a maze of dirt roads and past porches tacked on the sides of hills. The lights of the car outlined discarded cars, buses, and rusting engines. They passed a caravan where someone tried to grow a few flowers to beautify the drab surroundings. Mario's house nestled into the side of a hill.

'Here's my dugout. Come on in,' Mario invited his voice softly intimate. 'Would you like to shower first or a drink?' Mario leapt from the wagon and ran around to the driver's side, and opened the door. With a slight bow, he took Gillian's hand and led her from the car.

Uncertain, Gillian looked at a lean-to built across the face of the hill. It's not very flash, she thought; Mario would have had a better house than this.

What she saw almost took her breath away when she stepped through the door. Tiles paved the floor of the lean-to. A white wrought iron table and chairs sat in the middle. Two glass sliding doors led into a beautifully fitted out kitchen.

Mario directed her through the kitchen into a comfortable lounge with velvet drapes indicating a window but which covered a dirt wall. Two double glass doors led off either side from the lounge-room to what she presumed were bedrooms.

'Make yourself at home.' Mario invited as he moved close and placed his hand on her cheek. 'I'll get Sam and put him to bed.'

To break the tension, Gillian remarked, 'your house is beautiful. Opal mining must pay.'

'If you come in with me, you too can have more than this.' Mario's breath brushed her cheek, and his nearness was unnerving.

Gillian suppressed a shudder. Instinct told her she was on dangerous ground. But her starved heart and battered self-confidence drank in Mario's offer of romance.

'You are a beautiful woman. You don't need a man who is a drone. You could go far. Together we could take the world.' Mario took her into his arms; his breath fanned her cheek. The moment broke as Gillian pushed him away and stepped back. What they were doing was not right. She had promised to love Sam 'until death do us' part.

'Where is Sam?' she whispered, trying to calm her fast-beating heart. 'I'd like a drink, please.'

Mario stared at her; suppressed anger firmed the lines around his mouth as he moved toward the kitchen. The little fool, he thought. I'll teach her who the boss is.

Left alone, Gillian took notice of her strange surroundings. Fancy living underground like a rabbit, she thought, amazed. It was so fresh and comfortable. A blast of air came through the roof, and looking up, she could see a small cluster of stars and realised that fresh air funnelled down a shute on top of the hill. She walked around, examining ornaments and furniture. It was a room of luxury and gave Gillian cause for thought. She and Sam should leave. They had no business being here. This man was not what he seemed. Well, what did he appear? Gillian felt confused and realised she was in over her head.

Mario re-entered the room with a tray placing it on a low table.

'This coffee smells fit to die for,' Gillian smiled coolly, trying to distance herself, ' I'm exhausted. It's been a long day, and I'm not used to this kind of life. I'd better go and see if Sam is all right.'

'Not so fast, Gilly, you and I have some unfinished business,' Mario said as he moved to face her. He placed his hands on her shoulders and drew her to his body.

'You honestly don't think you can escape me so easily, do you?' Mario's voice was soft with desire. His dark eyes flashed with passion. His fingers dug into her flesh. 'I am not a man to be denied what is rightfully mine. If you want my help to find opal, you must pay me with more than money or opal. You are a gorgeous woman. I think you find me attractive also.'

His voice was husky, and it sent shivers up and down Gillian's spine. Then suddenly, his lips clamped over hers. She could taste blood as his teeth bit her lip. He savagely tore at her blouse.

'Get away from me.' Gillian panted, struggling to free herself, beating at Mario's chest with her fists. She kicked at his shins. 'Let go of me, you animal!' She grunted, but her struggles only served to arouse him.

He laughed at her puny attempts. 'You're a real fighter, aren't you? But I will win.'

She tried to slip through his grasp, but he was too quick, and he caught her in a headlock. She thought she was going to choke. 'Sam!' she croaked.

The sudden change in Mario had taken her by surprise. He's been so charming and attractive, and now he was like an animal, a real live Jekyll and Hyde. Helplessness and terror swamped her, robbing her of strength and thought. Where was Sam when she needed him! It was the story of their life.

'Sam won't help you. He's out for the count. I've seen to that,' Mario growled.

'What have you done with him?' Gillian screamed, trying to make a run to the door. Mario grabbed her wrist, picking her up and flinging her down onto the lounge, throwing himself over her body.

'He was out of it so far that he didn't see me. I've spiked his drink.' Mario's grin was triumphant.

She screamed, 'Sam!' as she brought her knees up to push him off. He had her body pinned with his legs while his hands tore at her top, exposing her breasts. 'Sam, Sam, help me,' she screamed,

A blow from Mario's fist snapped her head to one side, and for a moment, she was stunned and lay motionless, flitting in and out of consciousness. Then, as violently as a massive body had imprisoned Gillian, she was freed.

'So that's your game. Raping unsuspecting and helpless women,' growled Sam's voice. 'Ravage my wife while I'm sleeping, would you?' A massive fist crashed into Mario's face as Sam turned Mario to face him. Gillian heard the crunch of broken bones as Mario's nose flattened across his face. Blood sprayed Sam's singlet. 'No one harms my wife,' he bellowed in rage.

'She asked for it,' Mario sneered as he wiped the blood from his eyes, 'You should take some lessons on how to keep your wife.' A knife suddenly appeared in Mario's hand.

'Lookout, Sam. He's got a knife.' Gillian gasped; her eyes wide with terror.

Rage filled Sam like raging fire. His reflexes were slower these days, but his karate training in his youth had become second nature as he roamed around the world for a couple of years after university. Immediately, he was back in attack mode, waiting for the right moment to slip past

Mario's defences. Sam's foot shot out, connecting with Mario's wrist, the knife went flying. Sam delivered a punch, and Mario sagged to the floor like a bundle of wet washing.

Surprise had caused Gillian's mouth to fall open like a hungry fish. She couldn't believe that this man was the same person before her and the Sam of a few hours ago. She had last seen him passed out in the station wagon.

Sam pulled off his dusty, sweaty and blood-soaked singlet and pulled it over her head to cover her nakedness. 'Come on. Let's get out of here before his nibs come to.' Sam grabbed her around the waist and half-carried her out to their wagon. He opened the passenger door; picking her up, he thrust her into the seat then struggled behind the wheel, taking off with wheels spinning, throwing up a cloud of dust.

A quarter of an hour later, the neon sign of the Umoona Motel loomed up off to the right. 'Mario said there were no other motels around,' Gillian faltered, her lips already swelling.

'That crook would tell you anything just to get what he wanted,' Sam barked. He drove the car up to Reception. 'Just wait a minute while I book in.' Sam slid from the wagon and disappeared inside. A moment later, he was back.

'Our room is around the side here. It will be out of sight of the main thoroughfare. I said you weren't well and needed peace.' No sooner had he cut the engine than he was scrambling from the wagon, grabbing their bags, and trotting as fast as his short legs would go. He dumped their bags inside the room then hurried back to the passenger-side door. He helped Gillian inside and sat her in a lounge chair.

'Here we are, love,' he said breathlessly. 'You'll be safe here.' He propelled his overweight body to the fridge, tumbled some ice cubes into a towel, and gently placed it on Gillian's face.

She cringed in pain. 'Stop fussing, Sam. I'm all right. But thanks anyway.' She held the towel in place, grateful for his help. Her legs felt like paper; her nerves were as tight as violin strings. She couldn't believe Sam had it in him to understand. He had never cared for her in this way since their honeymoon. She revelled in his attention. This man caring for her was the old Sam of pre-marriage days. She realised that she had slowly assumed responsibility for both over the years, leaving Sam feeling he had no part to play in their lives. Tears welled up at what she had done to Sam and what had nearly happened to her. Yet he had shown another side of himself today, as he dealt with Mario. A violent characteristic he never showed anyone until today when she was in danger.

'You need a shower, ducks.' Sam took her toilet bag from the case and led her to the bathroom, and helped her undress. 'Look at your sunburn,' he cooed as he gently soaped Gillian's battered body and stood her under the shower. 'You need something for that. I heard cold tea does the trick.'

He carefully dabbed her dry and placed a clean nightie over her head. As she lifted her arms above her head, the movement brought a groan to her lips. Sam kissed her shoulder tenderly.

'You're killing me with kindness, Sam. I don't deserve you.' Gillian said weakly through swollen lips as he settled her on the bed. 'Mario did turn my head with his charm. A little voice kept urging me to be cautious, but I kept comparing him with you. I was so wrong; you are twice the man he is.'

'I know Mario got to you. You thought I couldn't see, but I noticed. I knew he'd spike my drink. Even though I was tipsy, I could still think clearly enough to know he was up to no good. Things are going to be different from now on; we've both made mistakes, it seems.' Sam looked tenderly at his wife. 'I thought I'd lost you.' Sam's voice was hoarse with fear.

He busied himself, boiling the kettle and making tea. He took two Panadol from the packet in the first aid kit in their bags. How could I have let this happen? Sam thought. I've let myself go physically; I'm off the drink and into training again from now on. I might even offer to become a trainer at a gym. I've been blaming Gill for over-riding me all the time, but I took the easy way out and became a couch potato. That's finished now. Gill's the most precious thing I've got, and I'm going to look after her. I don't know what I'd do without her.

As he sat on the edge of the bed looking at her, he said, 'Gill. I want to apologise for being a right bastard to you over the years.' His hand trembled as he handed her the cup of tea and the painkillers.

Gillian didn't reply, but she gave him a pitiful smile. With shaking fingers, she took the cup, slopping some of the contents down onto the bed. Sam guided her hand to her lips, and she took a sip and swallowed the pills.

'I'm sorry you had to go through all this. I'm sorry, love.' Sam repeated.

'Oh, Sam,' Gillian hiccupped. 'I was so scared.' Her blue eyes filled with tears at the memory of her ordeal.

'Don't cry, ducks.' Sam's arms went around her. She lowered her head to his shoulder and sobbed out her fear and pain. Sam's chin rested on top of her damp hair. His heart withered like a dried apple with shame over his past failures as he held her shuddering body.

As her tears subsided, he declared, 'Gill, I'm giving the booze away, and I'm going back into karate training may even become an instructor. Never again will I put you in such again.'

'You didn't tell me you trained in Marshall Arts? When did you learn?' Gillian was intrigued by the new side of her husband. Sam had never talked about his youth, and she had never asked. 'It was in the past,' he'd once said, 'let it stay there.'

'After I finished university, I drifted around overseas, so I needed to learn how to survive.' Sam shrugged.

Sam had made promises before and never kept them, but Gillian believed this new man.

'We'd better get some sleep now.' He rose from the bed and settled her down, adjusting the pillows and tucking the blankets around her shoulder. As he watched her eyes close, he thought she's the only one I've ever really loved. She has given me so much, and I've given her so little. He bent over and kissed her softly on the brow, then took a shower.

Through the lather of shaving soap, he muttered to his image. What can I do that will make up for my neglect? A secretive smile played at the corners of his full lips as an idea occurred to him.

The next morning, Gillian heard Sam's gravelly voice coaxing her back to the real world. 'What's the time? It must be late,' she yawned, noting the sun was well up. Its beams played across the floor, and dust motes danced in the air.

'Ohhh, am I stiff. I can feel every muscle in my body.' She tried to sit up but fell back with a groan. Her body felt like a thousand knives were piercing it.

Sam subsided onto the bed beside her. He leant over and propped her up with more pillows and made sure she was comfortable. Then he shyly passed a small parcel into her hands. 'Here, ducks, for you.' A huge smile split his face in two.

'What's this?' Gillian said, surprised, as she turned the parcel over. Sam was behaving in a most UN-Sam- like manner.

Gillian almost laughed out loud at the roughly wrapped package of gold paper and the crumpled golden bow that spoke of Sam's handiwork. His efforts to impress her melted her heart. He might have been her knight in shining armour yesterday, but today he was her bumbling Sam.

'Open it!' he demanded, hardly able to contain himself with excitement.

Gillian pulled the wrapping off and gasped when she looked into the fiery red heart of a large opal ring nestling in the blue velvet-lined box.

'Why it's my birthstone,' Gill's voice registered surprise. She looked at Sam; she had underestimated him. Tears filled her eyes; she loved Sam.

Sam had never felt as bad as he had yesterday. But he'd never felt as good as he did at that moment watching Gillian. Her pleasure and awe mirrored on her battered face as she gazed at her birthstone.

Gillian carefully took the ring from its bed of velvet and passed it to Sam. 'Here. You put it on my finger.'

Sam's thick stubby fingers fumbled to get the ring on her slim finger. His love knew no bounds at that tender moment.

'It must have cost a fortune,' she said, looking up at Sam in awe. At that moment, she realised the depth of his feelings for her.

'Nothing is too good for you,' he replied. 'I can't live without you, Gil,' he said, kissing her pink nose. 'The thought of losing you leaves me cold.'

Gillian leaned over and drew Sam tightly to her. Their cheeks together, they basked in a cocoon of wonder at having found each other again.

'Are you feeling better?" Sam mumbled a few minutes later.

Gillian released her headlock on him and replied, 'Yes. Why wouldn't I feel good with the bravest husband in the world?'

'I'll help you dress and pack,' Sam offered, jumping off the bed. He pulled out a fresh pair of undies. Selected a pair of shorts and top and put them on the bed.

'Oh, no, not those old things,' laughed Gillian. 'I'd better wear a dress to go with my opal. Anyway, what's the rush?'

'We've got a plane to catch.'

'A plane,' Gillian echoed. She wondered if Sam should be certified for the madhouse.

'Yes. We're off to the Gold Coast for a week.'

Her mouth rounded into a startled O. 'B...bu... but...what about the station wagon? We can't afford a holiday.'

'Sold the wagon,' declared Sam complacently. 'Got a good price for it too; seems like there's a shortage of good cars up here. It's paid for our holiday. We haven't had a holiday in years. This will be our second honeymoon.'

Gillian threw back the blankets and leapt into Sam's arms. It occurred to her, as Sam swung her around laughing, that her horoscope predictions had come true. She'd found romance, been through the trials of adventure, and the birthstone was riches beyond belief.

A new day! A new life!

GWENNETH LEANE

EMMY JANE'S GONE MISSING

The coach rolled to a clanking halt
Amid the dust and yapping dogs.
Men raced to horses sweating flanks
Grappling with harness, chains and buckles.

From the coach in straggling lines
Passengers discharged, disgruntled
The stout, the thin, the tall.
Children fretted at their coat tails.

Escaping flies and heat, the weary travellers
Trooped into the homestead tavern
Seeking sustenance for aching bones
And respite from the jolting ride

Above the din of entry and departure
'Where is my Emmy Jane? She's missing.'
A frantic mother ran in circles
Searching for her darling girl'

The coach into the distance faded
The mother's weeping broke the silence
She rocked in grief among the homestead workers
And found no ease amid their solace

RAINBOWS ACROSS THE OUTBACK

All through the night
The searchers called for Emmy Jane
Dawn peeped between sparse mulga trees
With heavy eyes and hearts they rode

Days stretched like empty years,
The nights were filled with nightmares.
The grieving mother lost all hope
Overwhelmed by dark despair.

At last! At last! A cry was heard.
'They're bringing home the girl.'
There was no joyous shout or buoyant step
For in their arms she lay as cold as stone

Into the mother's outstretched arms was laid
The tiny body thin and dried
Tears dripped from hoary chins
As toughened bushmen cried.

Today out on the Birdsville track
Amid the dunes and crumbling ruins
Iron railings and a headstone mark
The resting place of Emmy Jane.

GWENNETH LEANE

THE GREENHORNS

Children ran every which way, many of them in just their birthday suit. They were to sit on the floor at the front of the hall so they could see, but no-one took any responsibility for them, and they ran amok. Crocodile Dundee was showing, and the whole town attended.

The building, a tin shed, was called the Progress Hall. The noise level was rising; soon, the roof would lift off.

My husband Bruce and I had seen the film before in more civilized circumstances. Because we were new in town, we decided to attend.

The miners wore thongs, shorts and navy singlets joined by the women who came clad in shorts and cotton tops, the opal field's fashion.

We sat in the middle row, isolated by our dress, age and teetotalism. No one knew us; perhaps no-one wanted to know us. We were in a cocoon surrounded by noise, beer, colour and activity. We gave up on the film to watch real live Dundee's of the opal fields. Far more entertaining.

We were on the opal field to peg claims. In their great wisdom, the Mines Department thought the only fair way to allocate the claims was to revert to the Victorian goldfields' practice in the 1850s. On a designated day, the mining engineer of the opal field fired a shotgun into the air. People then rushed off to grab a piece of land 50m by 50m and peg it, hoping that underneath was the precious opal.

The day before the designated day, everybody and his brother arrived in town. Tensions were running high. Some miners camped on their claims to ward off claim jumpers. It was illegal to put any pegs in until after the gun went off.

We intended to stake a claim; it was on the edge of the central area. We, like everyone else, had patrolled the field and made our choice.

The blast from the gun echoed across the hills and valleys; we hurried to our claim and began to measure and drive in pegs.

We experienced a surreal moment when out of the scrub appeared a Toyota 4WD with two khaki-clad Mines officers. 'Have you got a licence?' they barked. 'Yes, back at our camp.' We replied civilly. 'Bring it to the office before closing time today,' another shortly delivered order. These men were the modern equivalent of the goldfields' hated troopers, just another way to show the divide between them and us.

While trying to fit in on the opal field, we met some Korean miners. They were hoping to strike it rich; the town existed because of fortune hunters.

We discovered the Koreans shared our Christian faith, and they invited us to share in their service. They even asked my husband to preach at one of their services.

Their English was limited, and our Korean nil. The language barrier proved a wall too high to build friendships.

Eventually, the Koreans returned home with their fortune, and we too followed later. When riches are realized, the fly-by-nights leave. Only the die-hard opal miners and their families remain.

GWENNETH LEANE

Murphy's Station

Squeak, squeak, the rocker swung like a pendulum
Murphy sat in blue despair, he'd failed to keep the trust
The iron fist of drought gripped fifty thousand hectares
He reached out for his trusty gun

The water dried to blood red mud
Carcases rotted on the banks
The stench of death filled the air
Black crows and eagles fully gorged could hardly fly

The moneylenders threatened to foreclose
Their jowls of fat shook with glee like a gobbler's wattles,
Murphy's heart smashed to shards, he was a broken man
At his shoulder waited the spirit of his ancestors

Storm clouds bubbled into black mountains
Brassy skies turn funereal grey
Murphy stood, his rocker stilled, the gun back on the wall
Rain drummed a tattoo on his roof.

RAINBOWS ACROSS THE OUTBACK

GWENNETH LEANE

MURPHY'S PRAYER

When the crop turns blue
Old Murphy's in a stew
His dollars will be few
Soon he'll sleeping on a cold bare pew.

So he's looking to the sky with many a sigh
On his lips a prayer so shy
No cloud forms on high
His farm remains stone dry

His heart in dark despair
From his farm he'll have to part unfair
In his heart failure is like a dart
His grandfather's inheritance just a farce

Like dark ships of fate clouds sail across the sky
The rain tumbles down in feet
Water turns the road to a river of red
Crops have been lost

RAINBOWS ACROSS THE OUTBACK

The dams are full the ducks begin to breed
The crop begins to mould and turn black
There'll be no fat ears of wheat.
The hearts of Murphy and his Missus bleed
Murphy's seen the earth gasp
For moisture to ease the rasp
He knows it'll heal and grow so fast
So he'll stay and keep his Grandpa's trust

GWENNETH LEANE

MURPHY'S COOK

The cook was in a bleedin' fume
Because his stew had grown a bloom
His bread had risen like a rocket
Breaking shearers teeth right at their socket

The shearers in full voice complained
With knife in hand and deadly mein
The cook reduced the men to jelly
They slunk away on empty belly

With hunger eating at their guts
Up to the homestead door they ducks
'Another sheep we'll never shear
Unless we're prop'ly fed and given beer

'Now men,' ole' Murphy pled.
'I'll see you're prop'ly fed
There is 'nt any need for flack
Just shear my woolly backs

RAINBOWS ACROSS THE OUTBACK

The cook was young and female
There'll be trouble without fail
As through the rafters
The smell of burning toast did waft.

'You blokes had better sit and eat
Before the meal is at your feet
At any flack from youse, I'll not falter
Cos' I'm 'ole' Murphy's daughter'

'The boss has gone too far this time',
The shearers swearing was sublime
'We're outa here and far away
Our footprints on this floor will never lay.

GWENNETH LEANE

MURPHY'S NEMESIS

Black smoke billowed on the far horizon
Murphy watched in consternation
His eyes mere slits
He stared and wondered what was left

Bushfire! His nemesis, seared his mind
He must push his cattle to the river flats
From the homestead steps he jumped
Yelling for his trusty Heeler

The old fire truck spluttered into life
The Missus leapt onto the running board
She rode it like a cowboy on his bronc
Every gate she opened wide

The Heeler ran with snapping jaws and vicious teeth
Amongst the cowering cattle
With snapping teeth from the Heeler
The cattle broke their daze and ran

Red dervishes of flame leapt high
Defying Murphy's watery spray
Retreat he must to the homestead
To save just what he could

With blackened face and reddened eyes
Old Murphy and his Missus
Surveyed the blackened land
They'd saved the homestead just
Hungry cattle bellowed out a starving song.
Floorboards creaked as Murphy prowled
Along the homestead veranda
He looked within himself he'd have to start again.
Could he get up again and wrest a living from the land?

From deep within the answer came
'You've been through drought and flood and won
You've got the courage of a David
This is your land, your place, you'll stay.'

GWENNETH LEANE

KEEPERS OF THE FENCE

The Great Wall of China is used as a comparison to understand the immensity of the Dog Fence; never-the-less, it is an Australian icon.

The Dog Fence snakes 2,250 ks in length across South Australia, dividing the State in two. The Fence as a national barrier begins on the cliffs of the Great Australian Bight at Nundroo and drunkenly wanders across South Australia, New South Wales into Queensland to end near Goondiwindi, Queensland. Total Fenceline is 5,300 ks.

The first cells of the Dog Fence were being built around 1850. Individual properties were Fenced, then later groups of property owners joined together to make their collective properties vermin proof.

The pastoralists moved ever northward and southward, looking for better grazing. Their leases grew ever larger. It became apparent that the sheep industry would fail before it even started because of the dingo's predations. Many solutions were used to combat the wily dingo, but with no success, and so the Dog Fence was born.

Len Burton was the first Dog Fence Board Inspector and the longest-serving inspector. Before becoming inspector, he had been a boundary rider looking after fences for local Boards. When the Dog Fence Act came into being in 1946 and proclaimed in 1947, Len became the first Government Inspector. He served as Dog Fence Inspector from 1946 – 1964-65.

Len would go out and do a section of the Fence using a string of camels. It would be a reasonably steady pace with the camels. At the end of his allotted section of Fence, Len would make sure a town nearby could post his reports. Then he would do another length of Fence and repeat the exercise.

Eventually, Beaucracy decided it would help Len to do his job quicker if he had a vehicle. The first vehicle for Len was a two-wheel drive. The car was useless in the rough terrain like an aeroplane sailing on the ocean in a storm. After World War Two, when jeeps were two a penny, a jeep was bought for Len. Then later, a Landrover replaced the jeep.

Initially, no one gave much thought to the fact that Len should be able to cover the sections of Fence much quicker. Bureaucracy asked no questions, satisfied in having provided mechanisation for Len. So Len continued as he had always done. Driving along the Fence, camping a week here, a week there, make his reports and posting them off. Len never changed his work habits, nor did the speed of inspecting the Fence.

Bureaucracy failed to understand that he should be travelling faster than when using the camels. How he fooled Bureaucracy provided a good story for Len to tell after he retired from the Service. There are places along the Fence known as Burton's Camp, and a little hut on Lake Frome's edge referred to as Burton's Rest.

Another of Len Burton's tales comes from the era when time and distance held no value. Len used to rest his camels on Roopena Station just outside of Whyalla. Even though Roopena was 500km from the Dog fence, it was close to transport and adequate water. Change over teams was kept on Roopena and became part of the Station stock. The idea was that Len would bring in one string of tired camels; another line of animals would be waiting for him refreshed and ready to go. Too restored, it seemed, for when Len was loading the new animals, they turned skittish.

The station workers warned Len, "Tie your gear down, or you'll lose it."

Len had hooks on each of the camels' saddles for every piece of equipment he carried. There were frying pans, saucepans, water bags, shovels, you name it, there was a hook for it. As Len saddled up the string of camels, they skittered and danced at every clang of equipment. Finally, something fell off with a loud clatter, and the whole line of camels took off, hell for leather. They bolted for miles down the track. There were pots and pans, groceries, cups, boxes, bits and pieces scattered from dinner to breakfast. It took a week to gather everything up and reload again. Finally, the camels were loaded, and Len was ready to make his inspection of the Fence.

The people whom the Fence draws to itself are larger than life. They live in Bryan's memory as he paints a picture of life along the Fence. Bryan believes their stories are part of the rich tapestry of Australian settlement and need preserving.

Before the 1930s, the Dog Fence was separate sections. During that era, the Fences were patrolled by boundary riders. These men spent endless lonely months working in harsh environments where one slip, one mistake often led to an untimely death. As the story goes, there was one such chap by the name of William Mooney.

Mooney's section of Fence ran from the South Australian border back toward the Simpson Desert. After a long stint on his part of the Fence, Mooney chose to slake his thirst at the Birdsville pub. Instead of blowing his cheque at the bar, William Mooney loaded his packhorse with two crates of Scotch whiskey and headed off back to his camp and begin his next section of the Fence. Presumably, he intended to make the whisky last out over the long weeks until his next visit to the town.

Six weeks later, a report came into the Police Station at Birdsville travellers found Mooney's body beside the track to Bedourie. When the Police investigated, they found Mooney's bones surrounded by empty whisky bottles. Mooney had made camp on his way back to his Fence section and opened a bottle of whiskey. He must then have become so drunk that he forgot to hobble his horse correctly. In the morning, when he came to, there was no horse.

Mooney knew what his fate would be under the circumstances, so he steadily drank his way through the whisky until it was gone. By then, death had claimed him. Mooney's grave can still be found just off the road to Bedourie, Queensland.

As a manager, Bryan found lots of things done that were not part of the job specification but were part and parcel of caring for the Dog Fence's human face. Bob Wiles was one of the human faces in need of care. Bryan and his wife Helen took Bob to live with them, and he spent many years as part of their family.

Helen describes Bob as tough as fencing wire, as enduring as the Fence itself. When Bob worked on Malbooma Station, he'd come into the homestead in his old Land Rover to get his supplies. He was seventy years old then but still working on the Fence. His policy was an honest day's work for a fair day's pay. He began his working life at fourteen with an old bullocky.

Apart from working on the Dog Fence, Bob was a general handyman. One of his jobs was to look after the water supplies. He believed his forte was to keep the pump jacks going and in the summertime, keeping the pumps working was a dire necessity to keep the station thriving. Bob was in his element.

An A-Lister Junior engine operated many of the pump jacks at the time. It was a big stationary engine that had a sizeable solid pulley. When the machine opened up, it thumped a steady choof-choof day and night like a beating heart running a marathon. There was a leather belt going from engine to pump jack. Leather stretches and from time to time must be adjusted to keep the traction. Special belt dressing was available for the job, but Bob had a better idea for keeping the belt tight.

Bob's miracle solution was treacle. It worked very well accept that when the honey-like liquid gets hot, it crystalises into sugar. It was usual to go out on a bore run after Bob and find the engines thumping away surrounded by billowing clouds of smoke and the belt stationary. The pulley was slipping on the sugar and the pumpjack swamped by black bull ants having a banquet. Avoiding the ants and switching off the engine was hazardous. First, petrol had to be drained from the station Ute's petrol tank to make a torch and burn the ants away. Then repairs could be made on the machine, and the belt replaced.

Bob and his miracle treacle became such a problem that the station manager barred the storekeepers from giving Bob any sugar cane product. Bob referred to the product as Gooley gum.

"Give us some Gooley gum," he'd say.

"What's Gooley gum?" The storekeeper would say.

"That golden stuff in tins. It's good for slipping belts."

"No, you can't have any of that to use on belts."

"Why not? It's perfect."

Bob's workmates despaired because they had to check the pumps after Bob's inspection trips, knowing they would find treacle plastered everywhere.

After Bob died, his daughters arrived looking for him. The Lock family were glad to be able to introduce him posthumously to his girls. The sad thing was they had left it too late to find him alive.

It was something of a surprise to find he had married and had children. Everyone presumed that his wife grew tired of living in the bush, or maybe something happened to disillusion her so that she left Bob. To bushmen like Bob, city life terrifies them, and they could or would not fit; there was always the question: what would they do in a city. So the men stayed in the bush, and their wives and children left.

Bob Wiles may not have won any medals, but he has a place of honour in bush lore. To pay tribute to the old Fencers like Bob is to tell their story.

GWENNETH LEANE

THE DAM BUILDER

'Struth! We've landed on the backside of the moon,' Red Stevens exclaimed as he and Barry Menz stepped on to the graded dirt airstrip. Mail and passengers visited Andamooka from all corners of the globe, an opal mining settlement in the remote north of South Australia. The Cessna aircraft flew in three times a week.

A large clay pan was utilised as an airstrip about 8 kilometres from the town. A drunken tin shed on the edge of the airfield used the name of the terminal waiting room. Barry looked around bemused.

'Crikey! There isn't a tree in sight! It's just red gibbers and saltbush, as far as you can see. This place is no place for us Red, let's get back on the plane now before it leaves.'

'Hang on, mate, let's stay put until the plane comes in again in a couple of days. We might as well see what makes the town tick now we are here.' A strong wind blowing across the airstrip whipped up sand, stinging Red's legs beneath his shorts.

'Let's go and get a beer,' Barry urged, 'I'll suffer sunstroke just standing here.'

'I told you to pack your sunblock and hat,' Red grinned, adding, 'there is a sign down there that says Opal Oasis; that must be a pub. Let's go and see.'

'Hey, you blokes, the mail truck's got to come out for the mail. You can get a ride into town then. It's a fair hike. Have you got hats and water? Where's your sunblock? The pilot yelled above the roar of the plane, the engine gunned for the take-off.

'When will that be?' Barry's voice drowned in the revving engine, dust and wind.

'We might as well start walking,' Red picked up his travel bag.

'What! Walk eight kilometres in this heat? You've got to be kidding!' Barry stared in disbelief at Red. But rather than be left alone surrounded by nothing, he picked up his bag and followed. That was Red, jumping in with both feet, never stopping to think about the consequences.

'Whose mad idea was this to come out here to the backside of nowhere?' Barry grumbled, brushing flies from his eyes continuously. 'We'll die of thirst before we reach that pub. I don't feel too good.' Red glanced at Barry and saw that, indeed, Barry was sweating and pasty-faced. In a panic, Red looked around, but there was no shade, just an endless, desiccated landscape.

'Hang on, mate…' Red began when Barry collapsed. Red rushed to Barry's side and stood, so the sun was blocked. Red took from his bag the paper he'd been reading on the plane and began to fan his stricken mate while fumbling for a mobile phone. The town was still a dusty smudge on the horizon.

'Look, here comes the mail truck now. Hang on, mate.' Red began waving his arms, driven by fear, even though there was no need.

The truck drew up beside the two men, and a battered hat poked out of the window.

'What the hell are youse two doing out here? Don't youse know ya can die of thirst? What's the matter with yer mate?'

'The heat's getting to him, and we haven't any water.'

'Stupid city slickers; come out here unprepared,' growled the mailman, grabbing a canvas water bag from the front of the Toyota and a pannikin, dribbled some water onto Barry's lips. Wetting a handkerchief, he wiped Barry's face. The lukewarm water revived him, and he sat up.

'What happened?'

'You collapsed, mate. I thought you were dead. I was just going for the undertaker.' Red quipped, but beneath the jocular attitude, there was fear and memory of his failure and near demise.

With the mail man's help, Red assisted Barry into the Toyota.

'Hang on, mate; I gotta pick up the mail from the airstrip yet. A stiff whisky will give youse a lift.

A dust pall hung over the town from unpaved roads the scribbled between low hills. White mounds of mullock looked like some underground creature had been busy burrowing. What appeared to be verandas built into the side of low hills were shelters of underground dugouts where a few people lived to escape the heat. Blowers stationed at the base of several mullock heaps blew dust tails into the air. These machines were improvisations that sucked up dirt and stone from underground in a similar manner to a vacuum cleaner. The soil was spat out on top of the ground allowing one man to operate alone down a shaft. The pulse of generators and rattle of bulldozer track somewhere in the distance was constant background music. The suffocating heat blanket was settling over the town even though it was still early in the day.

'Here you are, Rusty'll fix you fella's up.' The mailman pulled up in a cloud of dust in front of the pub. 'I gotta drop off the mail bags at the Post Office next door.'

Barry, supported by Red, staggered into the pub and dropped into the nearest chair.

'What's the matter with him?' Rusty Adams, the hotelier, looked at the two men, 'A drink is what you two need.'

Rusty placed ice-cold glasses of water on the table before the men. They sat silently, sipping their drink, absorbing the coolness of the bar. The realisation came home to them that their reckless actions had placed them in a dangerous position. Memories of Red's accident filled their minds, and respect was born for the territory in which they found themselves.

'Any place we can get a bed for a couple of nights?' Red wiped his mouth with the back of his hand.

'Yeah, I got two single rooms for ten bucks a night. There's also the Andamooka Motel a bit further down the road, but they charge like a wounded bull.'

Rusty Adams leaned on the bar spreading his brand of good cheer.

'We'll take the rooms.' Red delved into his shorts pocket and produced a ten-dollar note.

'I think a beer would be the order of the day, now,' Barry looked meaningfully at the pub keeper and fetched his wallet from his back pocket.

'I'll be in that,' Red agreed.

The pub keeper drew the beers, saying, 'Here are your keys. Your rooms are just down the passage, two doors on the right,' and unhooked the keys from a board behind the bar and threw them down on the counter.

'Stayin' long? He asked, looking the two men over. They seemed an odd pair to be mates. Red looked like he'd dressed in the dark, while Barry looked a regular playboy. The female hearts in Andamooka would beat a tattoo at one look at Barry with that lock of blonde hair falling over his forehead. 'City slickers' was written all over them, and only cowboys like these two would think of walking eight kilometres into Andamooka with no hat and no water.

'Yes. Might do some mining.' Red's face was turning the colour of his hair with the heat and alcohol, an empty stomach and a fright. His manner said no questions, please. His recent past was something he wanted to forget. That was part of why he was in the backside of nowhere, trying to get his life back together after the accident. He hadn't bargained on another mishap so soon.

'No!' we're leaving when the mail plane comes in again. I'm not staying out here any longer than I can help after passing out with sunstroke, Barry asserted.

'Don't be so dramatic, mate. You're OK now. Give the place a chance.' Barry could be such a drama artist.

'What do you blokes do for a living?' Rusty inquired. Every bit of information extracted from theses 'townies' would soon be relayed around the settlement. Tonight there'd be plenty of custom dropping in to see the two 'townies.'

'We're civil engineers between jobs,' Barry answered.

'We want to do a bit of opal mining for some recreation. Know any good spots?' Red chimed in.

'Well, if you want to mine,' Barry turned to Red irritated. The man never listened. 'You can do it on your own. I'm going home on the next plane. If you had any sense, you'd come as well.'

Ignoring Barry's comments, Rusty spoke to Red,

'Yeah, as a matter of fact, I own a mine. I'm looking for someone to work it for a percentage of the opal when found. I can take you out to German Gully where the mine is for a look before you decide.'

'You're on.' Red stood back from the bar. 'C'mon, Barry, get rid of your beer and let's go and see our fortune in waiting.'

Barry, a cynical twist to his thin lips, rolled his brown eyes ceiling wards, 'Here we go again. Off on a goose chase, only to find the goose has flown.'

Red followed Rusty out to the dust streaked, battered Toyota 4 WD, a disgruntled Barry trailing behind. They turned off one rutted track onto another track equally as rough and dusty where a car door stood propped up at the two roads' junction. 'German Gully' was daubed on it with an arrow pointing to the right.

'What's with the name, German Gully, Red asked, 'Did a German live out here or something?'

'Yeah. Two Germans gouged for opal for a couple of years, and then they found a million dollars. They must have gone back to Germany, 'cos we never saw them again. Maybe someone got to them and threw them down a mine shaft and took their opal.' Rusty shrugged as though he didn't care what happened to them.

'Each new area,' he continued, ' that gets opened up, is given a name. Like up the road a bit, there's Lunatic Hill, that's because you got to be a lunatic to gouge opal out there.'

'Did the owner find any opal?' Red was anxious to know his chances of success.

'Nah! When he didn't come back to his camp, his mates went out to see what had happened to him. He was dead by the time they dug him out. Here we are!'

Red and Barry got out of the Toyota, looking around at the treeless. Saltbush covered low, rolling hills.

'What damned awful country.' Barry muttered.

'Yes. Where's the mine?' Red turned 360 degrees, trying to find some feature in the landscape.

'If you don't watch it, you'll fall down the shaft,' Rusty grinned as he thought of the fun he was going to have with these two city slickers. He reached into the back of the truck for the miners' hats.

'Put these on and press the button on the hat, so we've got a light.' Rusty said as he put on his hat. Turning, he climbed down a rickety, perpendicular, iron ladder into the bowels of the earth.

'You blokes gonna stand up there all day?' Rusty's voice floated up to Red and Barry. They moved to the lip of the shaft and stared down at Rusty's pinpoint of light bobbing twenty feet below them.

'You first,' Barry nodded at Red.

'Yes, that's right. I can break my silly neck first.' But Red swung onto the ladder and began the descent. Gypsum sparkled from the walls of the shaft, caught in the light from their hats. Tunnels branched left and right in search of opal seams.

'I've been working in this drive. I need a partner to help me. In the winter, when it's cooler, everyone comes up from the city to mine, so the pub gets pretty busy, and I don't have time to get out there. In the summer as now, it's too damned hot. I found some colour in this drive the last time I was here. With another blast, I reckon we'll find some opal.'

'I'm not a mole,' Barry complained. 'Neither are you, Red.'

Red ignored Barry. As an engineer, his business was to study strata and ground formations. He had noticed vertical seams in the walls. His memory stirred; he remembered reading about how opal formed and where it lodged.

'Yep, I'll give it a go. What's the deal?'

'You'll what?' Barry couldn't believe his ears. He hadn't bothered to look around; it seemed a pretty dangerous sort of a way to mine with no shoring up of the earth. He kicked at a stone in frustration. What would it take to make Red listen to common sense?

'I thought 60 per cent for me and 40 per cent for you. I'm finding all the equipment etc.' Rusty offered, 'Do you want a contract?'

'No! You look an honest sort of a cove.' Red put out his hand, and the two men shook.

Barry couldn't believe that Red could be so naïve; he shook his head in disgust.

Over dinner that evening, Red rehashed the new venture. I reckon we might be onto something. Did you notice the fault lines running through Rusty's claim? He's been digging in the wrong place. I didn't think it a good idea just yet to tell Rusty what I saw. Rusty seems pretty generous with his percentage of 60/40. Did you know that opal comes from hydrated silica – silicon dioxide?'

'You wish! I didn't see any fault lines, and you're a bloody fool not to get a contract drawn up. If there is any opal Rusty could do you for your share,' Barry warned. 'All I saw was hard work, heat, flies, and being diddled out of my share, and what's more, I don't care how opal forms. All I know is I'm not going to get sucked in with opal fever, and you would be wise not to catch opal fever yourself.'

'You're a wet day in Melbourne.' Red leaned back in his chair and looked at Barry. Since his accident, Red's attitude to life and to Barry had undergone a dramatic change. He'd decided there were many things he wanted to do with his life, and listening to Barry telling him what to do and not do wasn't one of them. He'd always respected what Barry said, but now it was time to be his own man and follow his dream.

'I think I might accept Rusty's idea of taking over the old miner's cottage across the toad. It's a bit basic at the moment, but I could make it comfortable. It won't cost me a cent.' A dreamy look settled over Red's face. 'There's something about being in an outback town that makes one feel they are on the frontier of civilisation. Maybe it's because it's so harsh and rough and different from any place I've been. It'll be a challenge to live with only the basics.'

'What! Are you turning philosopher now? Maybe the heat's got to you as well,' scoffed Barry. Red was not responding as he did of old. What was happening?

'I'm just saying what I feel. Wonder what Anna would think of it out here,' Red wondered.

'Don't wonder any more. Anna'll hate it.' Barry snapped. 'You're not seriously thinking of living in that hovel across the creek that they call the main street, are you?' Barry was incredulous. What would Red be doing next?

'We-e-ell, it's free.' Red justified himself as he began to doubt the wisdom of living in the rundown shack, yet it appealed to him to live with just the basics and be innovative in restoring the cottage. It was a challenge that he wanted to accept. 'It'll be cold at night. It's close to the store, post office and pub. I know it's a bit under the Ritz, but I'll be out at the mine all day.' Red admitted to himself that he wanted a good excuse for using the derelict miner's hut.

'I've found false starts too many times, Red,' Barry looked at Red accusingly. 'I've learnt not to trust anymore.' Barry liked to make Red squirm over their accident by hinting that it was Red's fault.

The bridge's collapse only served to separate the two friends further, even though Red had recovered. The old order of friendship would never be the same again. Barry was trying his utmost to preserve the old order when he was boss, and Red followed. Red was no longer responding as he should, and it left Barry on shifting ground, which was a scary feeling.

Barry was wrong, Red thought; he had learned that he didn't care about the same things as Barry any more during weeks of rehabilitation. Red wanted to move on with his life, even if it meant living out here in the desert and roughing it for a bit. Red also knew he'd carry the responsibility for those two deaths to his grave. Barry seemed to have forgotten their mates had died.

Barry now insisted the design calculations were faulty, which meant a fault in the plans. In blaming flawed models for the accident, Barry accused Red subtly of being responsible for their mates' deaths. Red checked and rechecked the plans time and again and couldn't fault them. He didn't understand how or why the bridge collapsed. It was the weight of responsibility and guilt that had led to his nervous breakdown. He could sense that in the raw frontier town, he'd be able to heal and become a man again, not an image.

Red lay a moment collecting his wits, thinking that the thunder he could hear was the result of a hangover from the night before. As the locals arrived, the two mates told and retold their story to the accompaniment by fresh rounds of beer.

A clap of thunder overhead brought him upright, and he knew it didn't belong to his hangover. Lightning lit up his one-room dwelling dug into the creek bank that was also the main street of Andamooka.

The last thing he had remembered last night was seeing Barry propped up against the bar, yelling, 'I'm not going to stay in this hell-hole another minute. It's your fault I nearly died of sunstroke yesterday. You talked me into coming, just like you always do.'

'You didn't take too much persuading. Anyway, you didn't have to come,' Red hiccupped, 'you told Anna I was a 'has been' and I couldn't fight my way out of a paper bag, and you had to come to see I didn't do something stupid. Well, you must be in the same paper bag to come out here with me if you didn't want to.'

'That's right, mate, you don't know your backside from your elbow, and you call yourself an engineer,' Barry sneered, his tongue loosened by too many beers. 'No wonder the bridge collapsed.'

'Shut your lying mouth, or I will,' Red yelled and lunged for the taunting, handsome face of Barry Menz. Toppling over onto the floor, the two men rolled around, punching each other. Two patrons managed to part them without attracting any punches to their bodies.

'You can't ever allow me to forget one sorry minute of the disaster, can you? You have to tell the world. You kept nagging me until I broke down, then you started on Anna, trying to get her to leave me,' Red shouted, a green fog of jealousy blinding him. 'You want Anna for yourself.'

'Temper, temper,' Barry taunted, 'that temper always gets you into trouble; they didn't call you red for anything. With hair that colour, you could light the whole town up.' Winding Red up was heady stuff, and Barry didn't always know when to stop.

Red broke free from his captors and rushed at Barry through the beer haze, intent on rearranging his face for good. Red raised his fist, and before he could connect with Barry's face, something slammed into his midsection. He felt himself drop to the floor and couldn't remember any more until now when he woke to the raging of the storm.'

Deciding he'd better investigate, Red swung his feet out of bed into knee-deep water. 'Crikey! Where did all this water come from?'

Even as he stood there bemused, more water poured into his hut. It broke across his sleep-fogged mind that he was in danger. He waded to the door and peered out into a black void filled with the roar of the storm.

As flashes of lightning broke the pitch darkness, he could see bits of rubbish, scraps of furniture, dogs, cats, unsecured water tanks and debris of all kinds rushing past him. What had earlier been the main street of Andamooka was now a raging torrent.

Red knew it was too late to wade through the racing water. He'd become part of the wreckage speeding down the creek. Since his near-drowning when the bridge collapsed and subsequent breakdown, he couldn't face being underwater. Fear reared its ugly head as another wave of water surged into his hut. Something bumped against his leg feeling around by the occasional flash of lightning, he discovered his goods and miserable bits of furniture were beginning to float.

The old miner who first built the hut had dug into Opal Creek's bank to get away from the heat with no thought of what might happen if the creek flooded. Red had no idea what had happened to the old prospector; no one seemed to know. The life of a fossicker was pretty hard out in the desert. It was easy to perish and not be found.

The dugout housed a bed made of four posts in the ground along one wall with Hessian pulled tightly across as a mattress and on which he'd laid out his newly bought bushman's swag of which he was so proud. A few other bits such as an old meat safe hanging from a rafter, a kerosene lantern standing on a shoulder of the earth on which the beams rested, told of the old timer's occupancy. The dirt walls, plastered with mud then whitewashed. A piece of hessian had been nailed across the roof to give the impression of a ceiling.

Coldwater swirled around him, creeping up to the knees. The stench of the place reminded him of a sewer. He remembered placing a torch on a shelf in the wall above his bed during the day as he prepared the dugout for habitation. He waded across to where he thought the flashlight should be, tripping over a chair on the way; he swore silently, now soaked with filthy water. As luck would have it, he found the torch by a flash of reflected lightening.

The feeble light of the torch allowed him to climb onto a chair and poke at the ceiling. Not a hope. He remembered the miner dug the room into the bank, and there'd be metres of earth above him. He waved the torch around, of course, the chimney hole! He splashed across to the stove and climbed up onto it.

Bits of rusted piping, soot, birds' nests, and dirt showered down on Red as he began to dismantle the flu. The hole was too small for Red's barrel chest and broad shoulders to squeeze through. Mud and water poured down off the hill above the dugout and through the hole, drenching him, filling his eyes and mouth with muddy water. Spluttering, he cast around for an implement to widen the gap. He'd seen an old rusty crowbar just inside the door. He dropped into the rising putrid water and waded across to find the bar. He wondered why the old miner hadn't made a way of escape; maybe it hadn't rained whilst the more senior man lived here, or he had drowned. Despair twisted his stomach like a piece of barbed wire.

Fear and water licked at him. I hope this is a nightmare, and in the morning, I'll wake up, and nothing will have happened, Red thought. It looks as though Anna's going to be a young widow and my two kids fatherless. Red didn't give himself much hope of life after the flood as he chipped away at the limestone roof.

"I'll bet Barry is tucked up in the pub sleeping it off, leaving me to drown. Just like when the bridge collapsed, wonder boy left me to die and ran off to console Anna as soon as he could. Who needs an enemy when they have a friend like a Wonder Boy?

Bitterness pulled the corners of Red's full mouth downward. Wonder who brought me back here after the fight? Why haven't they remembered I'm staying here?

Red's thoughts kept time with his chipping; the flashes of lightning outlined the hole from above. He was thrilled to find the dirt roof was not as thick as he'd first thought.

In the dim torchlight, he saw the outline of a chair floating nearby and reached across and grabbed it, placing it on the stove to get more height and leverage. Red almost tipped over several times, but eventually, he managed to stand on the chair. The water gushing down through the hole helped broaden it as he chipped. He worked to enlarge the hole enough to drag his body through.

He could now reach up and wriggle through, it was precarious, and he hoped it would work. Red grabbed a floating plank and laid it on the chair and across to the earth's ledge supporting the roof. It made a platform to stand and get leverage to heave his body up through the hole.

Several times Red almost overbalanced into the rising water while trying to stand on the rickety platform. Grabbing hold of a beam, he steadied himself and squeezed into the hole. Finding handholds of rock that would take his weight, he heaved himself up enough to get his head out and emerge into the raging storm.

Thunder rolled over Red; lightning lit up the drenched landscape, rain slashed at him like a knife. He began to shiver from cold and nervous exhaustion.

Red decided he'd be better to go and find shelter at the motel; it was on his side of the creek. I'll have it out with Barry in the morning. I bet he left me to drown so he could cut it with Anna. Red stumbled, falling over several times, grazing knees and elbows, trying to find his way to a road that would lead him to the motel.

'Good grief!' The startled manager of the Andamooka Motel, Ian Lamont, exploded. He thought he was looking at a drowned rabbit when he saw Red standing at the door of Reception. 'What's happened to you?'

'I was sleeping in the old miner's dugout across from the pub. I just managed to get out in time.' Red's teeth chattered.

'Those old cottages ought to be pulled down. They're death traps; maybe now something will be done.' Ian said laconically and disappeared inside, only to reappear with a pair of soft pyjamas and dressing gown and towel. He shoved them at Red.

'The shower's round the back in the ablution block. Don't use too much water and clean up after yourself when you're finished. Here's the key to room 6, it's on the second floor,' Ian disappeared back into Reception.

In the morning, Red walked out onto the balcony overlooking Opal Creek. The elements were at peace after the rage of the previous night. The water had subsided, leaving behind sandbars, gravel spits, debris and pools of water. If the creek were used as a street again, it would need grading. Open-mouthed with surprise, Red watched people with tanks on board trailers drawn up to pools pumping water into the containers.

'Why is everyone out pumping water from the holes?' Red wanted to know as he sat down at a table in the dining room. 'I shouldn't think it was very hygienic.' 'Water is scarce out here, ' Ian Lamont was a man of few words. 'So every little bit helps.' When the mud settles, you can use it to wash.

Red was silent as he tucked into his breakfast, then, 'Water is pretty important out here, eh?'

'You could say that.' What sort of a dumb question is that? Ian Lamont wondered as he cleared away the dishes. 'I hope you only had a four-minute shower, mate? We're not connected to the damn River Murray out here,' Ian reminded Red.

'What do you do for water, then?' Ignoring his host's lack of hospitality, Red worried about the problem.

'A bore's been sunk outback. Water slowly seeps into the shaft. About 150 – 200 gallons a day. Not enough when the winter influx of people arrives. Seven wells were sunk along Chimney Creek hole about twelve kilometres away. Windmills were erected on the wells to pump up the water. A water truck delivers to homes when there is no rain. The rains only happen once in several years, and these wells all but dry up.'

Red's mind was working overtime on an idea. 'But first, I must have it out with Barry, the great one.

***

Barry's only memory before he passed out that night was hearing Rusty Adams saying to a miner, ' Get this city slob to his room to sleep it off.'

When Barry could open his eyes enough to greet the new day, his first need was for a drink. He had sworn off booze after Red's accident because, deep down, guilt was eating at him. He had purposely sabotaged the bridge's construction but hadn't bargained on two other men losing their life and Red surviving.

Barry believed that Anna suffered all kinds of hardship because of her illogical love for Red, who was unpredictable and a loser to boot. Barry was sure he could win Anna if Red weren't around. Barry felt that if Anna were his wife, she'd have a better life. Barry knew he was the better man. He straightened his clothes, rumpled from having slept in them. What a night!

'Do you always have to enter a room like a herd of elephants? What happened?' Barry groaned, holding his head between his hands to stop it from floating off his shoulders.

'Thanks to you, I nearly drowned,' Red accused.

'Nearly drowned? What a blessing. Anyway, what did I do?'

'You knew I was over in the miner's cottage. It flooded, and I had to dig myself out through the roof.'

'Me- left you there? Hey, mate, steady on. I didn't even know you were in the hut. I passed out. What's this about a flood? I've just woken up,' Barry grumbled, taking stock of Red. 'Hey, what's with you? You look worse than usual. Your shirt had a row with your shorts?'

'I've lost everything. I told you I escaped in what I stood up in,' Red glowered at his mate. 'Why don't I believe you; it was the same when the bridge collapsed.' Red would never forget the noise and cries of pain surrounding him as he lay pinned under a concrete section, unable to help the stricken workers.

'It was never your fault,' Red accused, 'you made out you were Mr Innocent and never knew anything about the accident. According to you, it was all my fault, but you were supposed to inspect the quality of the work done, but you didn't, did you?'

Barry closed his eyes, still holding his head, appearing to be in pain. Red was too close to the truth.

'Well, don't blame me. I had nothing to do with drowning you.' Barry hedged. 'It's a pity you didn't stop to think more. Then we wouldn't be in this God-forsaken hole, and you wouldn't have lost everything.'

Red shrugged his shoulders, Barry was as slippery as a snake, and there was no point in making a song and dance; he was alive, and that was all that mattered, and besides, an idea was forming in Red's mind.

'I've got a plan for this place. We'll build a dam up the creek to catch the water and save the main street from washing away and give the town more permanent water.' Red could feel a surge of adrenalin as the idea took hold. The two men had now wandered into the dining room of the pub.

'What's this about a dam?' Rusty Adams shoved a plate of toast at Barry and a glass of red liquid, 'This'll put hair on your chest.'

Barry turned green at the sight of the toast and pushed the plate away, downing the drink. 'What's this stuff?'

'Something to deal with a hangover,' Rusty turned to Red, 'what about you? Want something to cheer you up?'

***

'No! I'm off the amber liquid. I nearly drowned over there,' Red's anger flared up again, and he glared at Rusty. 'You knew I was over in the hut. Why didn't you warn me?'

'Great, Scott!' Rusty stared at Red. 'I forgot all about you, mate. I was fighting to keep the water out of the pub here. Didn't you see all the sandbags at the door?'

'You didn't remember me! I nearly drowned.' Red was fit to be tied. No one seemed to care what happened to him. He could have died for all anyone cared. Was his life so worthless? Perhaps. Red shrugged again. What did it matter anyway? He'd just get on with his life. Hopefully, he would find a purpose to live while out here in the bush.

'What were you saying about a dam when I came in?' Rusty persisted.

At the word dam, a chameleon change crossed Red's face.

'I've just realised the need for a more permanent water supply here. I wondered if it was possible to build a dam?'

'What about my mine?' Rusty bridled.

Well, I'll mine for you after we've built the dam,' Red offered an olive branch.

'What's this about 'we've' built the dam?' Barry queried. 'What about 'you've' built the weir?' Count me out. I'm going back to the good life.' In the back of Barry's mind, he hoped Red wouldn't heed his urging because he wanted time alone with the beautiful Anna to declare his love and woo her.

***

'I thought you and me, seeing we were engineers, with the help of the miners and their 'dozers and scrapers, we could put in a dam.' Red was almost pleading because he saw a project that could change the way the town lived. Maybe, if they could construct a catchment area for the Andamooka people, it would atone for two lives in the bridge's collapse.

'Read my lips, mate; I'm catching the mail plane back to the big smoke when it lands later today. I'm never coming back here.' Barry glared belligerently into Red's face.

'Come on, Barry, you're between jobs; it wouldn't hurt you to do something for someone else.' Red tried to appeal to Barry's generous side, though he wondered if Barry had any charitable streaks.

'I'm not cut out for this type of life. Flies for meat and dust for dessert, my clothes soaked in sweat until they stand up by themselves and no water to wash them or me properly. Not on your life.'

'Hey! I'm not happy about my mine not being worked. The only thing, a dam might be a benefit to the town, though. How are you going to pay for it supposing the miners agree to help with their equipment?'

'There is funding for developing the towns in the outback,' Red said, 'submissions must be made to the right departments. I'm pretty sure we'd get the necessary funding for such a project.'

Rusty and Barry hooted in derision.

'I'll give Anna your love and tell her you'll be home never. Mate, she's wasted on you.' Barry's mouth twisted in bitterness, he pushed away from the bar. 'I'm going to shower and clean up ready for when the plane arrives.'

Barry's mind revolved around how to win the beautiful, blonde Anna. She was princess Di and Lisa McClune all rolled into one. He had always loved Anna. Anna would have married him if Red hadn't arrived at the University with his big talk and lofty dreams. The three became inseparable as he and Red studied civil engineering, and Ann sought a degree in fine art. After Red and Anna had married, he had hung out with them, hoping to ingratiate himself with Anna and eventually win her away from Red. It had made his insides crawl when she married Red. Red was such a loser. This trip to Andamooka, going opal mining, and now dam sinking proved it.

Red hesitated, torn between going home with Barry and staying here. He suddenly wanted to see Anna and his two kids. To feel their arms around him telling him they loved him and wanted him home. It was tempting to follow Barry.

But the people here are different. They gouge for opal under extreme conditions and always come up smiling, he thought. I want to make life a bit easier for them. Besides, I could live here. The thought startled Red; he had not thought he'd be compatible with the area and its people. The harsh terrain and raw lifestyle challenged his comfort zone; he realised he needed the challenge to find healing again.

As Barry left the room, Red's blue eyes followed him; I'll bet he doesn't give Anna my love. He'll do his best to win her away from me instead.

'Well, I'd better go back to the dugout and see what I can salvage.' Red walked out of the pub. His suspicions about what Barry might try to do in his absence uppermost in his thoughts.

***

Silt had built up in front of the cottage, and until it dried out, he could not enter the dugout. So he looked into the room through the hole in the roof. What he saw made him sit down on the nearest boulder and hang his head between his knees.

Red's new swag lay crumpled on the Hessian bed under a layer of mud. The stove resembled a rusting iron box and would never fire up again. Most of his pots and pans had floated away; they were probably resting in the middle of Lake Torrens if someone hadn't found them and taken them home as replacements. His clothes were a soggy mass. The silt was a veneer over everything. Maybe I can wash the mud out of them, Red thought as he took another look and then decided maybe not. I won't be able to live here anymore. I should have gone home with Barry.

Yet in the back of his mind was the thought he would find healing for both mind and body amongst these people, who accepted him on face value, so unlike city people.

Red returned to the hotel, where he and Rusty spent the rest of the day huddled over rough drawings of the dam that Red proposed a few kilometres up the creek above the town.

'Where in the name of goodness do you think you are going to get enough water to fill the flamin' dam?' Rusty wanted to know first off.

'Well, it rained cows and bulls last night; I nearly lost my life, remember? No thanks to you lot.'

'Oh well...' rusty shrugged, not wishing to discuss Red's near-drowning. 'If you're that keen we can organise a public meeting and put the idea to the people. But don't be surprised if it gets the thumbs down.'

The following evening the townspeople began to filter into the pub, agog over Red building a dam. Rounds of beer were circulated to grease ideas and persuade miners to agree with the dam's plans.

'We don't need a dam here. We'd have to pay rates and taxes then.' An old miner yelled.

"Why change? We've done without a water supply this long; why bother now," asked another.

'Can't you see that with a dam, you'd have water for longer periods? You could have gardens, your fresh vegetables, not sad, limp stuff that comes up by truck once a week from Port Augusta. Take a proper shower. Trees could be grown in the streets.' Red was nearly purple with frustration.

'What do we want flamin' trees in the street for?'

'Shade, of course, you drongo and to make the town look better,' Red yelled, aggravated at such a short-sighted attitude.

'Don't call me a drongo, I'll punch out your lights,' the old miner got up and thrust his face into that of Reds.

'Sorry mate, sit down and have another beer on me,' Red apologised. 'Let's talk about the dam in detail. I've got some plans here.' Red spread out his rough plans on the bar.

'Now see here...' but the old miner stomped off outside in a huff. Red saw he'd riled the crowd, and his idea for the dam was about to fold up. But Ian Lamont spoke from the back of the room,' I'd like to see a dam built. I can't make people care when they take showers at the motel. I've put up signs for care to be taken with water, but I might as well save my breath for all the good it does. So I'd like better water supplies.'

The crowd saw Ian's point. They began to see how it would make their lives more comfortable with water on tap. At the moment, people were hauling water nearly every day or paying someone else to transport it. Sometimes it was pumped from clay pans into tanks after every rain.

'Where will the dam be?' Someone asked.

'How will the dam be built?' another queried.

'I reckon Brooks Creek would be a good site.' Red explained that each of the heavy machines owners could take turns each day working on the dam wall. 'We'll apply for a grant that's available to remote communities.

It should only take a couple of months if we all get stuck into it. You blokes shouldn't lose too much time from your mining.'

A feeling of optimism spread across the meeting as men discussed how to build the dam's wall. Six-packs of beer were broken open. The dam was soon constructed and full of water, at least in theory, under the power of a glassful of golden, frothy beer. Everyone went home pleased with what they had accomplished.

Red spent the next few days surveying the site. Red's first challenge was to find appropriate material to build the dam wall. There was no hard rock earth anywhere within kilometres. Finding a quarry from which to cart rock and soil could be an expensive drawback. The venture was proving to be a challenge and consumed Red's every waking thought. With the hard work and mental stimulation, he found he was at last healing.

***

A few days later, returning dog-tired from the dam site, he entered his room. Throwing his cap on the bed, sitting on its edge, he pulled off his boots. He went to the fridge to find a cold beer and stopped short when a husky voice behind him said,

'Aren't you going to kiss your wife?'

'Anna! What are you doing here?' Red swung around in surprise. 'You didn't tell me you were coming up. When did you get here? Where are the kids?'

Red looked at his beautiful Anna, afraid to touch her if she wanted to tell him Barry had won her love. He needed to hold her, to bury his face in her soft hair, and smell the tangy perfume that she used.

'I left Darren and Kristy with Mum. She wanted to have them for a few days. She said I was silly to come all this way without letting you know. But I wanted to surprise you. They'll be here Friday; Mum's bringing them up on the bus.' Anna explained.

'You're Mum! You mean she's leaving the city and venturing into the great unknown?' The sudden turn of events left Red bewildered. He might have cut loose from his old life, but it didn't mean that those around him had to do the same.

'Darling,' he croaked, drawing her to him carefully, holding her, savouring her lavender perfume and the feel of her, burying his face in her shoulder. 'It is wonderful to see you. I didn't expect you to come all this way. The conditions are terrible. We had a storm here a week ago, and I nearly drowned.'

'Red!' Anna was horrified,' how did you nearly drown?' Anna stood back from Red, waiting for his explanation. After Red had related his story, Anna flung her arms around his neck, 'Oh, Red, I've missed you so much. I wanted to be a part of what you were doing up here. I wanted to see this place for myself.'

Red hugged her again with more vigour, forgetting how dirty he was. 'My darling!'

Her blues eyes peered out from under her lashes, enticing him with messages to be interpreted only in the bedroom. 'Don't break my ribs; I've only just arrived. Reserve my demise for when you get tired of having me around. Have your shower, and let me show you the house that I've rented.'

'OK', Red began to undress, leaving a trail of clothes behind him as he went toward the bathroom, 'Did you just say you've rented a house!' Red caught his breath. Anna wouldn't be staying long enough to rent a house if she was leaving him? She'd want to get back to her job at the art gallery where she worked, the shops, and the fun things she did with her friends.

'Wash your ears out when you shower, Red. I intend to stay as long as you do.'

'Oh, Anna, you don't know what it means to me to hear you say that. But what about your job?' Red emerged, dripping wet from the shower, to hug her tightly. He was still afraid to ask about Barry and what he had said and done.

'No matter how exciting my job at the gallery is and I love it, it is no replacement for you. I missed you, Red, more than I thought I would. I've never been so far from the city, and I'm scared stiff I won't cope, but I'm going to give it a good try.'

'Anna, you are one amazing woman, and you'll cope just like you always do.' Red's voice was full of admiration.

'Look, your dripping water everywhere; get back and finish your shower,' Ann laughingly admonished him. 'I'm soaked as well.'

Red's heart lifted; he gave vent to his feelings in song as he scrubbed the day's dust off under the shower. His beautiful Anna loved him. Barry had not been able to win her with his charm.

Red emerged clean a short time later, dressed in a pale green casual shirt and fawn shorts and sandals, his red curling hair slicked down, the hard work and no alcohol had trimmed off his flab. Anna's toes curled in her shoes; Red was quite handsome.

'Now, where is this house you're talking about, Anna? I don't remember seeing anything that could be called a house around here.'

'It's that house over on that hill to the right.' Anna pointed in a westerly direction as they climbed into the battered old Toyota Red had bought cheaply to get about in. All Red could see were two large picture windows set on either side of glass double doors at the hill's bottom. The slope of the mountain faced with dark stones taken from the creeks around the settlement. The windows and doors set into the stone facing. An expansive terrace was dozed out and paved in front of the glass doors. A table and chairs stood in a shady corner. It looked luxurious in the fashion of the opal field to die for.

'Some Yugoslav built it,' Anna explained, 'he's gone back home for a holiday on the proceeds of his opal.'

Red was silent, taking in the structure and artistry that had gone into facing the dugout and making it a home with the eye of an engineer.

'How much is the rent?' He thought it probably would cost an arm and a leg, but he would not deny Anna any comfort. Just to have her with him was priceless.

'Nothing!' Anna was happy. 'The owner is glad to have someone come and housesit while he is away. Come on inside and have a look.'

Somehow when Anna was around, everything went like clockwork. Inside, there was an extensive lounge area with a bar in one corner. A door led off to the right to another room that was a bedroom and en-suite. A very modern kitchen, pantry and storeroom were dug even further into the hill. To the left of the lounge, another large room dug out and partitioned to make two bedrooms. The walls were all faced with stone like the outside. There were so many nooks and ledges for ornaments. Bare dirt divisions faced with coloured stones created feature walls. It would be cool in summer and warm in winter.

'What do you think, Red? Didn't I do a good job of finding us a home?'

'I always knew you weren't just a beautiful face. I wouldn't have thought there was such a house in Andamooka and for free.'

'That's because you were too busy being a dam builder,' Anna laughed. 'You need me to keep you in order.'

'Let's go back to the motel and have dinner,' Red suggested. 'We've got lot's to do if we want to camp here tonight.'

'We only need to make a bed up.' Anna pointed out, 'the place is fully furnished as you can see right down to cutlery and crockery,' and she flung open the cupboard doors, 'See!'

When Ian Lamont had served Red and Anna their dinner and left them alone, Red gathered his courage and asked, 'Have you seen much of Barry since he returned to the city?'

'He came around a few times, wanting to take me out. He said he wanted to make up for your neglect. But I'm a one-person woman and told him so.' Anna looked at Red, her blue eyes full of love. 'He wouldn't listen, and I had to make it clear I didn't even like him; Barry left in such a mood. I was worried that he might do something stupid then. Barry came around and offered to bring the kids up, but I was a bit scared to let him. So when Mum offered to bring them, I was only too glad to let her.'

A great breath of relief ballooned Red's cheeks; he pushed his chair back and grabbed her hand. 'We need to be somewhere else at this moment. I still have a room here at the motel.'

An hour later, they lay in each other's arms, sated with lovemaking. Red spoke, 'Anna, I love you so much. I don't want to hurt you or make life hard for you, but I want to build this dam for the people here; it might make up for the lives that I took when the bridge collapsed.'

'I know, dear heart. But Red, the coroner, found that that the prestressed cement supplied was inferior and poorly erected. The investigator cleared your name of any blame,' Anna caressed his face.

'I should have checked, though, Anna. I trusted the suppliers, and I shouldn't have. I'm taking no risks with this dam,' Red raised himself on his elbow and looked into Anna's lovely face, searching for any sign of disbelief.

Without so much as a flicker, Anna returned his gaze, 'you did all that any man could do in trying to save the men. They rescued you in the end; you've paid for the accident with your own health.'

Red lay down again and drew Anna into his body with a sigh. Anna's words were a balm. I've felt better every day, he thought, and now Anna's here; it will improve even more.

By the time Red arrived home from the dam site, Friday Darren and Kristy were out on the terrace watching for him on Friday night. They rushed him, shouting 'Dad!' It felt so good to hold their young bodies in his arms. He greeted his mother-in-law, and then he noticed Barry.' Hey, I thought you were never coming back to this forsaken country.'

'Well, I couldn't let Anna's mother come all this way on her own trying to cope with two kids, so I brought them up. Now that I'm here, I might as well give you a hand with the dam.' Barry was oozing playboy charm over everybody.

It was a festive dinner that night with everyone wanting to tell his or her story. Later, Anna took the children off for showers and bed. Red and Barry were alone.

'How're things with the dam?' Barry clapped Red on the shoulder as though nothing had happened. 'The dam seems to be going great guns, I hear.' A smile stretched Barry's thin lips without reaching his eyes. 'Now that I'm here, I can help you organise the miners. Organising is something I'm good at, as you know.'

Red almost choked on his lemon squash; you haven't changed a bit, you skunk! He'd never noticed before, but Barry always big-timed himself by making snide remarks about Red's ineptness to organise.

***

Next morning at the dam site, Barry swaggered up to Red, 'I'll start pushing up dirt on the dam wall, and you can see to getting the trucks moving out to bring in the boulders to stop the wash.'

'No, you won't.' Red replied decisively.

Barry was puzzled. Red had always been easy to manipulate. Barry found he could no longer read Red's thinking.

'You'll take the truck Barry and get a load of boulders from the quarry in the Andamooka Range. Take Joe Strzelecki; he'll show you where to go. When you get back, dump the load in the creek below the dam wall to stop erosion.'

Surprise wiped the smirk off Barry's face. It had been so easy to sabotage the bridge because he'd been able to rescind Red's orders. It was just unfortunate about the guys killed, and Red survived. Barry planned the accident to kill Red. This time it should be easier to sabotage the dam wall. He would make sure Red would be the one to go. Then Anna would be his.

'If that's what pleases you, boss.' Barry sneered, walking away with a shrug and smirk. A thought came to Red, he's a dangerous man, but he put the idea from him as petty.

Near the lunch break, Red was driving the roller backward and forward across the wall to tamp it down hard. Barry had delivered his load of boulders, tumbling them down the side of the dam wall. Red was horrified. I told him to tip them at the base of the wall, not down the wall's slope. They will cause a landslide like that. What's Barry thinking? He knows better than that.

A flash of memory of entered Red's mind of the big cement casting for the cross-section began to slip. That had been Barry's responsibility to make sure it didn't. Red remembered seeing the defect and deciding to question Barry. The collapse knocked him down, and only now did he remember. What had Barry been trying to do? Did he plan for Red to be crushed or drowned as he so nearly was? So he could claim Anna for himself? Barry's my best mate. We've been together since our uni days. I never realised that he hated me so much nor how crazy he is over Anna. Looking back, Red could see many things that he hadn't noticed about Barry's behaviour. Deciding to question Barry, he jumped down from the roller and walked to where Barry stood on the bank. It was then he noticed Anna standing below the dam wall in the creek bed, waving to him.

'What are you doing down there, Anna?' Red yelled at her, taking in her danger.

'I've brought some scones and coffee for smoke-o for a hard-working band of men sweating to make an inland ski-boat resort,' Anna teased, moving toward the men on the bank. 'I also wanted to inspect the wall to see how it was coming along.'

'Move up onto the bank of the creek, Anna. The wall might not be safe, yet.' Red ran down to her, urging her up out of the creek

A shout from the wall parapet made Anna and Red turn in time to see part of the wall beginning to slide toward them. 'Run, Anna run,' Red shouted and grabbed her hand, dragging her with him to escape the slide.

'Red, look out,' Anna screamed as a huge boulder bounced toward them, knocking them to the ground. A dry river of dirt and rock caught up with them and raced past them to settle a few metres further down the creek.

'Here they are.' A shout went up. 'Somebody get the nursing sister and ring the Flying Doctor.'

'Are they alive?' Men began to crowd around with spades and bare hands to free Anna and Red. Their bodies were carried up onto the creek bank and laid under the shade of some acacia bushes, and resuscitation began.

'Hey! Here's another body. It's Red's mate. He must have come back. I thought he left?' Someone shouted.

'Must've tried to save them, eh?'

A day later, in the Port Augusta hospital, where the Flying Doctors flew Red and Anna, Rusty walked through the door.

'What happened?' Red mumbled through swollen lips

'The dam collapsed,' was Rusty's brief reply.

'But how! I was so careful about everything. I wanted to make sure there were no accidents.' Red groaned, trying to look at Rusty.

'These things happen,' Rusty laid a comforting hand on Red's shoulder.

'Anna, is she OK? I haven't been allowed to see her.' Another groan escaped from Red from the pain in his chest.

'Yeah, mate, she's fine.' As Rusty spoke, she slowly walked through the door on crutches.

'Hi! Sweetheart. She bent over the bed, her face alight with love. She smoothed his hair back from his face, looking at him; livid bruises appeared on his face, and his leg was cast.

Red reached for her hand, grimacing in pain as he did so. 'You look a bit battle-scarred, my darling.'

'I've got a broken arm and numerous cuts and bruises, but I'm OK.'

'It's wonderful to see you alive, darling.' A great sigh escaped Red's lips, his eyes were damp with unshed tears, and a deep thankfulness bubbled up from within him.

'Yeah, mate, it's good to see you two alive. Your mate, Barry, didn't make it through, I'm sorry to say.' Rusty's withered face looked even more withered. 'He must have been trying to save you two and copped it sweet.'

Red looked at Rusty, his face closed. The questions Red asked himself would now be left unanswered, like did Barry sabotage the bridge to kill him? Instead, two other men gave their lives for him. He closed his eyes, his heart sad. He relived the moment when the dam wall was coming toward him, his one thought was Anna, and he flung himself over her. A flash of memory revealed Barry was standing up on the wall, a triumphant grin on his face, then all went black.

What a horrible thing to think that man's best mate could be a killer! The suspicion concerning Barry's loyalty would always remain, but what was the point of blackening his name now?

'Yeah, he must have been trying to save us.' Red's face showed nothing of the turmoil of his thoughts.

'Well, don't worry about the dam, mate. The miners have been repairing the damage; it will be finished when you get back. Then all we need is a thunderstorm to fill it.'

Another thought occurred to Red, hoist in his own petard. He wondered why he should think of such a hard thing when his best mate had just died.

HARD BITTEN

With teeth of iron
The drought grips soul and body

Starvation rattles bones
Of hungry sheep and cattle

Finance dries away
Along with water in the dams

His eyes turn heavenward
Old Murphy pleads

'Just let it rain before
too must leave the land

GWENNETH LEANE

TAKE THE WEEKEND OFF

Men become lovers of the desert, living and dying among the dunes. They are captivated by its beauty, awed by its immensity and challenged by its harshness. They have learned not to take the desert for granted. They are, at all times, prepared for the many moods that it presents to its lovers.

'Let's go to Birdsville for the weekend, just to get away from the station and live it up for a couple of days,' says the man.

The woman is relieved. She has been in the bush and hardly seen another woman for years. She will look in the shops, buy the kids some clothes, sit in the pub over a drink, and chat with other women. Maybe, she'll get a hairdo. Excitement churns in her stomach; a smile eases her face, and the withering lines of the desert air written on her face are smoothed away.

The children become animated. They dream of ice cream and lollies, maybe a make a new friend. The girl badly wants a new dress. The boy has asked for a gun.

'You're too young, son.'
'But you had one at my age.'
'That's different.'
'Why is it different?"
'Because it just is.'

The boy is bewildered by this adult logic. Why do adults pretend they are wiser than their children when they are often smarter than the parent?

He can't wait to grow up and be free of this claustrophobic ignorance that blankets his questing mind. Someday he'll find the answers to life. The woman's voice brings him back to reality.

'Put your things together that you want to take for the trip tomorrow, children.'

'Yes, we'll leave at daybreak and be in Birdsville tomorrow night.'

A dust tail curled lazily out behind the vehicle as the travellers sped across the waterless wastes, their thoughts anticipating lights, good food, drinks with many friends, and loud music.

A pink flush heralds the day. The desert is gentle, at peace. The distant breakaway hills on the horizon are a purple streak. A crow cawed, a dingo crossed the road in front of the speeding station wagon, seemingly to disappear into the red earth.

'We'll stay at the pub.'

'Yes, that would be nice. The kids can watch a video and then go to bed. We can then sit in the bar for a while.'

'You promised us, Mum, we could sit up late.'

'Tomorrow, son.'

'Aww, Da-ad'

'Now, you kids behave and give your mother and me a chance to enjoy ourselves.'

The boy's gaze flickered across the empty landscape, noting the claypans were not even damp. The new day had arrived and night surrendered to the sun. The mystery of the desert was turning into glaring brilliancy. There is nowhere to hide out here.

The boy glanced at his sister; her eyes slid away from his, a slight shrug indicated it was best not to fight parents, go along with them. Life is trouble-free that way. His sister was pretty but weak, accepting her lot without question. The boy knew of women who fought the bush, but they died by the hand of the desert.

The boy knew that life would become like the desert for him, a vast ocean of dunes if he is as accepting as his sister. He recognises that his mind would wither under a cloud of isolation. He is different. His mother and sister would survive out here, but at what cost to themselves. His gaze drifted across the plains, now shimmering in a heat haze. The wind rushing in through the window came from hell itself.

Saltbush and blue bush seemed to wilt under the blast leaving the bare ground red, white and grey. No patch of green soothed the eye as far as it could see. The boy could not remember when it had last rained.

The girl leaned forward,

'Mum, I'm thirsty.'

'Where's your water bottle?'

'You didn't tell me to fill it?'

'Do I have to tell you to do everything?"

'Mum, I'm thirsty.'

'Where is the water bag?'

'Was the water bag put in?'

The silence was deafening as they each looked at the other, and realisation dawned; they were without water. A silence fills the car, and they are isolated by their fear.

'You'll have to wait until we see a windmill or a homestead or until we reach Birdsville.'

'Dad, that might never be.'

'We'll be there in another hour.'

'Dad, I can't wait.'

You should have listened to your mother, girl.'

The boy couldn't remember anyone talking about filling water containers. There was that attitude again that parents knew best. Why can't they treat us kids like people? It's as if they think we are stupid, the boy thought resentfully. The boy knew there was no water on board; what if they broke down? He glanced out the window; harsh was the best way to describe the land now. Not a crow cawed or a lizard moved; no emus broke the skyline. Everything was in limbo until the sun went down and night took over. The boy regretted not taking the initiative and filling a bottle, even though Dad had said travel light. The words of an old ringer's gruesome tales of people lost in the desert rang in his ears. It couldn't happen to them, could it?

The engine coughed, the car coasted to a stop on the side of the road. The man turned the ignition key, the engine growled. Each urged the engine to fire, but its response became a weak growl. The heat caught up with them; it was overpowering. The man lifted the bonnet, looked inside, and fiddled with some coils, tweaked at nuts and fixings.

'Mum, I want a drink.' The girl whimpered

'Me, too.' The boy added.

The man and woman glared at the children; they fell silent.

'What's wrong, Ben?'

I don't know, can't see anything the matter, Cheryl.

'Are we out of petrol?'

'Nah, filled her up before we left.

Eyes, filled with worry, scanned the desert for tails of dust denoting another vehicle. Overhead, a metallic sky hosted a fireball; a single eagle soared high above the landscape.

The man and the woman glanced at each other, then away, trying to hide their dismay from the children. The boy wanted to shout at them that he knew what was going on. The girl talked to her doll, saying it wouldn't be long before they would be at Birdsville.

'I better go for help. You stay here with the children and don't leave.'

'Where will you go?'

The man searched the landscape for inspiration.

'Let me go instead. You may be able to fix the car; you're a mechanic. Then you can come and pick me up.'

'No, it's best I go.'

The man felt guilty he urged travel light. It was a mistake in this country. He should have seen to it they were better equipped. He knew what the problem was, but he couldn't tell them that he couldn't fix it. He must do what he could to save them.

'Dad, shouldn't we all stay alongside the car? That's what the old ringers say?'

Resentfully, the man thought the boy was too big for his boots. He is always telling me what I should do. He believes everything the station workers tell him and never listens to what I tell him.

'I won't be gone long. There's a turn off back a little way. It's bound to lead to a dam or homestead. It looked to be well used.'

'Dad, can I come too? I can walk a long way. I could help.'

'No, son, stay with your mother and sister. You're the man of the family. Look after them; get some water from the radiator.'

The desert settled about the man. His stride was purposeful; the day wore on, the heat sucking him dry. His shoulders drooped. His eyes dimmed. Around him, the mirages beckoned seductively. They were visions of oceans of water –blue water a million miles away. In the distance, a windmill shimmered. The man left the road and headed across the plain. His eyes glued to the windmill he doggedly stumbled along.

'I will not walk in circles. I will not take off my clothes.'

But it was so hot, and he craved for a drink. His tongue filled his mouth like cotton wool, and he couldn't swallow. Perhaps if he sat a while, he'd feel better. He was so tired. How long had he been walking? Hours? Where was the windmill? He'd kept his eyes on it all the time. Could he have missed it? The desert spread out around him like a vast empty bowl. He sat on the ground; he thought he was talking to his wife and children.

'I'm sorry to have spoiled your weekend, my darlings. In a minute, I'll get up and find that water. It's around here somewhere.'

It was more comfortable to lie down. The man slept, never waking.

The woman, the boy and the girl watched the man striding along the track. He became a mere dot on the horizon then dropped from their sight. The man's going left a significant hole, and they each felt defenceless. To fill the gap, the woman said,

'Better get the ice-cream container from the boot and get some water from the radiator, son.'

'OK, Mum.'

But the water was rusty and undrinkable. Coolants added to it. It tasted foul, and they felt sick after tasting it. This one lifeline denied them; they felt small as ants in the vast emptiness and even more unfortunate than a newborn creature.

'I want a drink, Mum.'

'Don't we all, girl?'

'Shut up, sis.'

'Children, don't quarrel, sit here in the shade of the car and fan ourselves. It will start to get cool in a little while. Daddy will soon be back with water. When we get to Birdsville, we'll have a nice long cold drink and a shower.'

The boy flicked stones across the road. The girl talked to her doll, telling it that soon Daddy would be back with lots of water.

The woman stared across to where the man had disappeared. She was willing him to return. Nothing moved; the heat shimmered across the plain. The flies worried their eyes and mouths. The hours passed

'I think we should follow Daddy. We can meet him halfway.'

'Mum, shouldn't we wait here at the car? Someone might come along.'

The girl watched the boy and the woman; flies lined her eyes, she no longer bothered to hunt them away. Her whimpering for water had ceased, and the doll lay limply in her lap.

'You're father is bound to on his way back by now.'

'Mum, all the Bushmen say stay by the car.'

'I don't care what the Bushmen say. What do they know?'

Not wanting to admit to the children that they were doomed, she wondered if it was better to die trying to save themselves or die doing nothing. She had been scared of the bush, always staying close to the homestead. She had heard stories of people getting lost by just walking over the sandhill a few kilometres away and never being seen again.

'Put your hats on. Suck a stone. It might help to keep your mouth damp.'

'Mum, if we stay here, we could hang a plastic bag under the car and drain the dew into it tonight and collect some water.'

'The old bushies have certainly filled your head with nonsense, son. No! We are going to meet your father.'

The woman picked up the little girl and doll and took off. The boy followed reluctantly, not before stuffing plastic bags into his pocket. The woman began to sing and urged the boy to follow suit, but soon the song died, and they fell silent, concentrating on taking one step and then another.

'Shall we put your dolly under this bush? We'll come and get it when we meet Daddy.'

How much longer could she go on? The little girl was so heavy, perhaps if she walked. She didn't want to admit she had lost the man's footsteps. Somewhere he must have turned off the road.

'Let's sit here and rest a bit, eh?'

'Let's try and find a tree or some bushes first. There looks to be some up ahead.'

The trio struggled into the sparse shade of a lone mulga and flopped onto the ground to lay like rag dolls.

The boy looked at his sister. She reminded him of a drought-stricken animal, all skin and bone, and he realised that she was facing death. His mother propped against the tree, eyes closed. She was beyond caring for them. The boy was saddened.

'I will not give in. I will survive this; I could yet save my family. I want to make some sense of life. I haven't even lived yet,' the boy mused; the old bushies had learnt how to survive by using what was around.

'They are survivors. I will be like them.' The boy hung on fighting against sleepiness, struggling to sit up; pulling the plastic bag out of his pocket, he tied it to a low hanging branch.

'Mum, we'll have some water in the morning. I'm collecting water. Hang on.'

There was no answer, and the boy lapsed into unconsciousness. The wind drifted across the desert; sand drifted against the bodies, half covering them. Night fell; stars twinkled from a velvet sky, watching the tragedy from afar. The cold woke the boy.

'Water.'

It seemed like hours before he mustered enough strength to get the bag off the branch. Disappointingly only a few drops had collected. He struggled with the temptation to drink it all himself.

'Sis, here's a drop of water. 'He laid a wet finger on her lips, but they were stiff and dusty. The little body was so still.

'Mum?'

Was he too late? He crawled to his mother and wet her lips, but there was no response. He couldn't cry; he was so dehydrated. Anyway, boys don't cry.

'Just wet your mouth. Too much water kills.'

The boy wet his finger and pressed it to his mouth. He tried to dribble a little into his mouth, but it ran down his chin; he was unable to swallow. Vaguely, he heard an engine, then a voice.

'Here they are. We found the mother and two children. Was there a fourth?'

'Only the boy.'

'He used his savvy.'

Rocking over the rough track in a 4WD, the boy returned to the station. He thought,

'It's not courage that conquers the desert but savvy. It's being prepared for whatever the desert throws at you.'

WHAT A BLOODY MESS

I could have avoided the whole bloody mess if only I had conducted the tour boat out on the river myself that day. Taking tourists cruising on the South Alligator river was usually my job.

Tourists were like a flock of sheep. You'd tell them one thing, and they would do the opposite. When your back turned, they'd be off getting lost, drinking contaminated water and yes, being taken by a croc. Working as a tour guide demanded strict rules are applied, or loss of life would occur. I boasted that I had not lost one tourist.

When I drove the boat, I insisted on the pain of death that nobody trail their fingers in the water. No one could eat and throw bits of food into the river. I insisted everyone sit down in case we struck a snag and sent passengers headfirst into the river.

I noticed that as soon as the boat idled along the river, it was trailed by several of the prehistoric creatures in the hope of perhaps making an easy dinner of some careless tourist. The drought had brought increased numbers of crocs into the river. Their in-land water holes drying up.

I oversaw servicing the boat making sure we never broke down midstream and putting passengers at risk. I made sure the engine turned over like a charm; a gun was hidden under the seat. The gun was my secret; even the boss didn't know. I ensured enough life belts for every passenger was stored overhead under the canopy.

A busload of tourists had booked a tour through Kakadu. The usual bus driver phoned in ill.

'You had better take the bus through Kakadu. Someone else can take the boat trip,' the tour manager decided.

Had I taken the boat out this day, there would have been no trouble. Firstly, I know where every snag, log and croc hole are in the river. Secondly, the tourists would have been sitting down behaving themselves and thirdly, I would have had the gun.

The tour guide was a new chum and didn't understand that tourists must be governed strictly and treated sternly. One insistent passenger stood to get a photo of a nearby croc. The unthinkable happened. The boat hit a snag, and the jolt sent the passenger overboard into the water. Before the stunned passengers and guide could react to the water churned and thrashed like a washing machine, and the passenger was gone. People just sat there, stunned at what happened. The wife of the vanished passenger screamed, 'Do something! My husband's fallen overboard.'

The driver reacted by throwing a life jacket into the water, it was a useless exercise, and he knew it. He felt he had to do something. He pulled his mobile from his shirt pocket and dialled base,

'We've lost a man overboard; a croc has taken him. There's no sign of him anywhere. We are snagged and dare not move, or the boat will tear, and we'll sink. Crocs surround us.'

Within minutes another boat appeared with Rangers on board. Carefully helped aboard the second vessel, the passengers were ferried back to base. By now, a third boat had arrived. The crippled ship towed back to the jetty.

The suffering woman continued to scream, 'Why haven't you helped my husband? Why don't you search for him?'

A female passenger approached the distraught woman, put an arm around her, 'My dear, to try and look for him will place too many people at risk. You can see how many crocs there are in the river. He wouldn't have known what happened to him.'

'Someone should have at least fired a gun into the water,' the wife stormed.

When the boats returned to base, the resort manager took charge of the now quietly sobbing woman, ushering her away from prying eyes.

She was taken by helicopter to Darwin, where she received grief counselling and overnight accommodation provided. The Tour Company notified her family of the tragedy.

The search for remains was finally undertaken. A croc was caught and transported to a croc farm. The pumping of the beast's stomach showed the remains of a human. A DNA test was taken and reported to be that of the unfortunate passenger.

A sealed coffin transported to Melbourne, where the man had lived. The DNA report was filed and sent to the wife to get closure over her husband's death.

No one asked for any further proof of the truth. The Tourist Company did its best to white-wash the tragedy and compensate for the accident.

I knew that the driver of the boat was a new chum, inexperienced at handling tourists. He should have had another man of experience with him. It was negligence on the part of the tourist company. They had got away with it this time.

Let's hope the Tour Company learnt a lesson, but I didn't think so.

RAINBOWS ACROSS THE OUTBACK

The dollar speaks loudly, and they will compromise passengers again. I decided to leave the company and find another job. I felt heartsick at what had happened. If I'd been there, the whole bloody mess would never have happened.

OVER MY DEAD BODY

'You'd have thought we'd found the Argyle Diamond mine.' Dot Marsden snorted her frustration, 'the way Maria and Nicki have turned on us.' She banged down a steaming plate of roast meat and veg on the table before her husband, Tom. The odour teased Tom's nose, making it twitch in anticipation.

'Maria told me that they have been here for years and found no opal, and we have only been here a few months and found a rich vertical.' Dot reached for another plate for herself from a side cupboard and sat down opposite Tom under a lean-to constructed from recycled sheets of iron covering the caravan side. The lean-to did service as a kitchen and living area.

'Yes! I can see they would feel a bit cheesed off at our luck. I suppose I might too if I were them. But that's opal mining. It's a bigger gamble than betting on the horses, it seems to me.' Tom agreed.

He looked at his wife critically; where's my cheery mate gone? He could no longer think of her as his dumpling.

Her round face was deeply tanned, and stress lines bracketed her mouth. Worry drew her brows together. Were there a few more strands of grey amongst the raven hairs? Her trademark of humour and good cheer had slowly evaporated over the past few weeks.

Her plump figure had slimmed down due to hard work and depression, and fears that she never voiced.

She hasn't lost her touch as a cook, though, even if all she has is a small gas stove in the van; Tom sighed as he picked up his knife and fork and attacked his meal with gusto. Between mouthfuls, Tom remarked, 'I thought it would be a bit of a lark to see if we could find some opal. But it's proved nothing but trouble.'

'Mmm, I thought it might be good to have a bit extra for our retirement, 'Dot agreed in a lacklustre voice, 'how wrong could I be?' and how lonely and scared, but she kept these thoughts to herself.

Tom grunted and took a sip from his mug of coffee.

'Everyone seemed so friendly when we arrived. It seemed a very caring and relaxed community.' Tom continued, 'Now, it's as if we've caught the plague. No one speaks or invites me in for a coffee anymore.'

Dot picked at her food; it tasted like straw. She didn't feel hungry these days. She tried to eat to keep up her strength. She looked at Tom, scoffing his food down, his portly figure honed by hard work. His dark features even darker due to outdoor life. Since his retrenchment stacking shelves in a Supermarket at night was the only job, he could find.

How can Tom act so calm? Dot wondered; she felt envious.

'It's so peaceful out here lifestyle out here, after the rat race in Melbourne,' Tom commented between mouthfuls. 'In Melbourne, its wet and cold but out here, blue skies and plenty of sunshine every day. The climate is perfect this time of year. If we were back in Melbourne, we'd be freezing.'

'Perfect!' Dot exploded, 'I don't think it's perfect. I hate the sun. Look, my skin is dry and withered, and my hair is dull and stringy even though I use rainwater to wash it. I cut my finger the other day, just a snick, and because of the mineral in the water, it's grown into a large infected sore. The nurse at the clinic told me to bathe it in rainwater.' Then another thought struck her, 'Besides, I'm not into this cloak and dagger stuff.' She sighed, putting down her knife and fork; the smell of the roast made her feel nauseous. 'I would never have thought of fibbing about where I was going or what I was doing at home. I've become the world's best liar since we found opal.'

Tom watched his wife from the corner of his eye. Her full smiley mouth set in a grim line. An open, friendly person, she now had to keep her thoughts to herself and be suspicious, even of the people who claimed to be her friends. The silence was agony to this outgoing woman. It's high time I got her out of here before she cracks under pressure, he thought.

Dot gazed out into the bright midday sun. If only we hadn't side-tracked to Mintabie but kept on going through to Alice Springs, she thought, her mind on the trip around Australia they had dreamed of for so long. The trip had met all their expectations until they stopped at Mintabie. They meant to stay overnight just to say they had been to the opal fields. Instead, they'd become caught up in opal mining and stayed, staking a claim. Tom had put down a shaft using a drill named a Caldwell drill after the man who created it. The hole was about a metre wide. He discovered a thick seam of opal. From then on, it had been nothing but trouble, people accusing them of claim jumping, someone had tried to break into their caravan, and their new friends deserted them.

'Don't worry, my dear,' Tom comforted her as if he'd read her thoughts at the same time hiding his misgivings, 'I'll try and line up the buyer tonight. When the opal is off our hands, we'll get on with our trip around Australia.'

'I don't feel like continuing with our trip; I want to go home.' Dot's words ended with a catch in her voice as tears threatened. It was true; riches didn't bring happiness, Dot realized, as she longed for Melbourne's sheltered lifestyle.

'There are too many eyes and ears in this place. We thought no one knew about our find, but it didn't take long for word to get out.' Fear threaded through her voice, 'we're the target of every Tom, Dick and Harry trying to steal our opal. I wonder how people found out?'

Tom was now really concerned; Dot was usually happy to roll with the punches. It was not like her to complain so bitterly and be so melancholy.

'In a small town like Mintabie, everyone knows everyone else's business. You can't hide anything, no matter how hard you try. We'll just put up with living in a goldfish bowl for another couple of days. So cheer up, my dear,' Tom patted his wife's hand, trying to comfort her. 'We'll be out of here day after tomorrow. I've no regrets about stopping off here to mine for a while, though.' Tom said philosophically, 'What's life if we don't take a risk or two?'

'I can do without risks, thank you very much.' Dot's reply was blunt.

'When we first pulled into the caravan park and set up camp under the old Myall tree, it was another world.' Tom remembered the excitement of being in a remote mining settlement. 'We'd never done anything so daring in our lives before. Life in Melbourne suburbia is very narrow, isn't it?'

'Just give me good old narrow suburbia.' Dot lamented.

'We certainly caught a dose of opal fever, well and truly,' Tom's words were cut off, 'You mean you did-' Dot interjected disagreeably.

'I was not prepared for the suspicion and fear that we've encountered by the community.' Tom continued, 'Well, I'd better get back to the mine and pick up the rest of our gear. See you later, sweetheart. I'll be as quick as I can.'

Tom rose from the table and stood behind her, bent over and kissed her on the cheek. A ghost of a smile crossed her face, and she patted Tom's hands in thanks for his concern.

Tom disappeared into the caravan, reappearing with a shotgun in his hand, feeding two cartridges into it. 'There, it's loaded. Use it if you have to.' Tom laid the gun on the table. 'When I go, Dot, you'd better lock up and put a bar across the door. I want to know you have some protection. I've let Benjie go. He'll warn you at least if he doesn't scare them.'

'He'll lick them to death rather than bite them.' A weak smile broke the stress lines on Dot's face.

Tom's eyes darkened with affection as he looked at his wife.

'What about you?' Dot returned his gaze, 'You too should have a gun.'

'I'll be all right. Don't worry about me.' Tom picked up his hat and thermos of cold tea and moved out to the Landrover.

She smiled as she watched him drive away in a cloud of dust. Tom has his funny ways, but he's a good man. He understands how I feel. He's not precisely Man of the Year with his thinning iron-coloured hair and the beginnings of a paunch, but he is as reliable as day follows night. We've had thirty-odd good years' together and raised three kids. Thanks to Tom's hard work, our house belongs to us. Please, God, don't let anything happen to him.

Dot didn't consider herself to be religious. Still, a feeling of foreboding filled her. The need to invoke the care of someone or something beyond herself or her husband was acute.

She cleared the dishes putting them into a bowl of hot water, and washing them. That's another thing wrong with this place, Dot grumbled to herself. The water is as hard and full of minerals and scarce as diamonds. I never thought I'd be saving the wash-up and bath water to keep a few tomato plants and pea vines alive. I must remind Tom to cart some more water from the bore tonight; I want to wash the clothes tomorrow before we leave.

Dot poured the water onto her precious plants growing in large urns just outside the door of the lean-to. She paused to look across the road to where Maria and Nicki Callas lived. Maria was outside hanging out washing. Dot waved, but Maria turned away. Tears welled up at the back of her eyes.

A distant generator thumped away like a heart, and the distant rattle of bulldozer tracks working a claim broke the silence of the bush. It's such a beautiful day; I wish I could go shopping instead of stuck home here minding the damn drum of opal stashed in the caravan. Anyway, there are no shops here, Dot thought as she re-entered the lean-to. They call the store here a supermarket, what a joke! They only sell essential goods. The bread and meat are always frozen, that is when there is any. The veggies are limp and stale, and I get treated as if I've got leprosy at the store. She sighed and looked around, noting all the things Tom had added to make it a comfortable room. I should be grateful, but I wish I were back in my lovely home.

She shivered as she turned and entered the lean-to going over to the lounge area and turning on the TV to fill in time. The reception was snowy, especially during the day, but they'd got used to snowy programs.

Dot was restless and uneasy; she could not forget the other night when they'd come home from a meal at the pub and disturbed someone trying to break into the lean-to. They had reported the incident to the Mine's Officer, Ian Flemming.

'Even if Ian did find out who it, he wouldn't arrest him. The thief could spin Ian any sort of yarn, and because he's a local, Ian would believe him,' Dot had raved at Tom. 'He's not going to arrest his friends.'

'Ian is a pretty fair sort of a bloke. He's never struck me as having favourites,' Tom disagreed, ' that's it! You're going to learn to handle a gun.'

'But I don't want to,' Dot protested. 'I hate guns.'

'It might save our lives.' Tom said practically

'Tom, I can't! The thought of it freaks me out,' Dot said nervously, her hands breaking into a cold sweat.

'Come on. We'll go out bush and have some practice.'

The next day Tom had insisted Dot go with him into the surrounding scrub. Tom had then taught Dot how to load and fire. She became reasonably proficient.

'You're not bad, Dot. You'll be a gold medallist yet.' Tom had praised. 'I'd better watch my step, or I'll be the one to get blown away so you can have the opal all for yourself.' Tom had grinned cheekily, trying to jolly Dot out of her dark mood.

'Tom! Don't talk like that,' she had snapped and had punched Tom playfully on the shoulder,

'Now I can rest a bit, knowing you can at least scare off an intruder,' Tom voiced his satisfaction.

Now, as she sat barricaded in the lean-to with Benjie lying at her feet, the gun seemed to have a power of its own. Dot's eyes were drawn to the gun where it lay on the table. I don't know if I can bring myself to use this thing. I hope I never have to use it.

Dot got up from the lounge chair to glance out of the window and froze to ease her tension. Was that movement in the scrub behind the caravan park laundry? She turned and looked at Benjie. His ears were pricked, listening, nose twitching, trying to read the sounds and smells. There was a Toyota parked down the road from the Callis's. It looks like Maria has visitors, she thought. What should she do? Try and raise Tom on his radio? He'd laugh at her if her fears proved pointless. Unable to settle, she tried to call him regardless, but there was no answer. He can't be near the Land Rover, she thought and hung up.

***

Tom's mind was on Dot as he drove out to his mine; he was well aware that prying eyes might be watching his movements. Even though they were staying in a caravan park, they were relatively isolated. There were only two other permanent residents, the Callis's and an old miner, in a dilapidated van. It would be easy to hide in the bushes near their van un-noticed.

He and Dot had been married for thirty years, but she still roused his passion. They were not so young any more, and their bodies were starting to sag south. But the romance was still in their relationship. I'll make it up to her when we leave here, he promised himself. So caught up was he in his plans, Tom did not notice the hungry gleam in Whiskey's grey rheumy eyes that followed the Land Rover heading out to the minefield,

Propping up the upright of the pub veranda was his favourite position. He could get a good view of the town and knew who was doing what and where they were going in Mintabie. What he didn't discern, he made up with incredible accuracy.

In his right hand was an empty beer can and his left hand held a cigarette. He'd just drained the last of his beer, and the need for another drink was dire, but he was flat broke, not an unusual state for Whisky.

Paul Marcos would be pleased with this bit of news, and he'd be assured of a good grog-up tonight. Whisky held the reputation of the dullest brain in Mintabie. Still, he did know that Paul Marcos was an expensive ticket for a drink in exchange for information.

Whisky also had enough grey matter to recognize that Marcos was using the information for fraudulent purposes. But Whisky believed if he didn't know what Marcos did, his conscience was clear. His one aim in life was to stay drunk to keep his memories at bay and the drink demons happy; after that, what happened to people he didn't care.

Tossing the empty can onto the road, Whisky left the veranda crossing the street to Paul Marcos' supermarket, opposite the pub, at a fast penguin-like waddle. A toothless smile of anticipation hidden under the grey stubble on his chin,

"'e's gone out to 'is mine. 'e's gunner pick up some more opal.' Whisky wheezed.

'Who's gone where, man? Explain yourself!' Marcos snapped from behind the checkout. The man smelt like a brewery. Most likely hadn't bathed since Adam was a boy.

The smile faded from the derelict's face, the rheumy eyes squinted as he stood hat in hand before Paul Marcos, 'You speak to me nicely, Mr Markos, or I won't tell you what I know.' Whisky's voice had changed into a little boy's whine, and he tried to stand tall and dignified.

'Don't you threaten me, you drunken old sot?' Paul coughed. 'Ugh, you stink! When did you last have a bath? When your mother last bathed you?' Paul despised the older man, but he used him to get information about the townspeople and who had found opal and who hadn't. Paul had a consuming passion for money to impress his family back in Greece. His elder brother was to inherit the family business and a large house. At the same time, he, as the youngest son, would receive nothing. By migrating and marrying an Australian woman, he had become the black sheep.

He didn't care how he went about getting rich, careful though to mask his shonky deals with a very public show of humanitarian aid to the community. He was President of the Mintabie Progress Association and the Social Club. Paul Marcos considered he'd done well in convincing the people of Mintabie that he was a good bloke.

'I'd catch me death.' Whisky shivered, 'Bathing is a waste of time and water.'

'What did you want to say, spit it out, man,' Paul tried to distance himself from Whisky by moving back from the checkout counter, but Whisky followed him like a bloodhound.

One day the high an' mighty Paul Marcos will get his comeuppance, Whisky's lip curled in spite. When I feel better, I'll show the thieving crook what I can do. Right now, I need a drink terrible and 'e's gonna give it to me.

'Tom Marsden's just gone out to 'is mine. 'e'll be bringin' in some more stone.' Whisky puffed. ' Must have a ton of it stored in 'is van. 'e's been cartin' bags for days.'

'You're kidding me.' Paul snarled. If he showed Whisky the slightest bit of leeway, the old drunk would string him along just to get more free booze. He was getting sick of paying for the old sot's permanent bender. Anyhow, soon, he would be rid of the older man. Then an idea struck him; he'd be burning his bridges behind him, but he was never going to return to Australia.

'I wouldn't lie to you, Mr Markos, 'Whisky bleated. 'Gawd's truth, I wouldn't. I saw Marsden drive past just this minute.'

Paul drew his wallet from an inside pocket of his coat, 'Here, get yourself a drink... and a bath.'

'Thanks, Mr Marcos, you're a very gen'rous man.' Whisky bowed his head subserviently, but before he vanished, he threw in another piece of information. It wouldn't hurt Marcos to know there was somebody else sniffing around for the Marsden's opal. 'That Abo, Billy, I saw 'im sneakin' 'round the Marsden's the other night. Thought you might like to know, Mr Marcos.' Serve Marcos right if somebody beat him to the opal, Whisky thought. He could taste the alcohol already and feel it burn his throat as it trickled down to his stomach.

Marcos watched Whisky scurry across the road like a rat on the scent of a feed. The earlier idea consolidated into a plan. He'd need to move fast if Whisky was right about the Aboriginal, and there was no reason to doubt him. It looks like I have three problems to solve. I'll start with Billy, the Abo. I'll stop him dead in his tracks, and I mean lifeless. I will not have anyone invade my territory, especially an Abo, not now when I'm so close to being a rich man. The Abos will only waste it anyway. I have booked to fly to Greece in two days, and then my big brother will have to move over. He was leaving his Australian wife and children. They could fend for themselves. There was always Centre Link for them to fall back on and get his kids later on. There were ways and means.

His thoughts were already in Greece and what he would do. Let his lazy, skinny wife do something for herself and the kids. She only stays with me because I'm a good meal ticket. Maybe I'll find a Greek wife. I'll prove to my dear parents I'm smarter than my illustrious brother. They'll have to respect me then.

He called his wife to mind the store, jumped into an old Ute, and then drove to the caravan park on the edge of town. Sitting still for a few minutes watching the park, he saw the Aboriginal staring absorbedly at the van. It was easy enough to sneak up on Billy. The look of surprise on his face when the knife went home gave Paul a sense of deep satisfaction. Paul knew of an isolated mineshaft out in the bush. It was his favourite dumping hole, and it didn't take him long to tip a bundle of old clothes down the shaft. No one would bother to look or even wonder what was down. Nobody was going to worry that an Aboriginal had gone missing. It would be supposed he was walkabout. Paul Marcos dusted off his hands, took off his coat and threw that down with the body and, now for problem two.

Calling into the pub, Marcos found Whisky on his third schooner. The look of bliss on his face turned to surprise when Paul addressed him peremptorily,

'I got a job for you, Whisky. Get in the Ute.'

'But Mr Markos, I 'aven't 'finished me drink yet,' Whisky whined.

'Get in the Ute, or it will be the last b... drink you ever see, let alone taste,' Paul picked up the bottle a put it under his arm. 'Come on.'

Whisky looked longingly at the schooner and then at Paul. He took a large gulp of beer then waddled after Paul like a penguin drawn to the sound of waves. They drove out along the road to Mimili, an Aboriginal settlement 100 kilometres west of the town. The bush track passed along the top of a rocky outcrop jutting high above the plain. At the highest point, Paul Markos stopped the Ute.

'Wot you got for me to do out 'ere, Mr Marcos?' Whisky's manner was meek, his eyes on the bottle of wine residing over the back seat. If he could just have a few more sips to quiet the rage of the demons in his stomach, he'd be able to concentrate on what Marcos was doing.

The bottle tucked under Paul's arm, he nodded to Whisky to follow. The two men stood on the cliff-top overlooking the Indulkana plains.

Neither was interested in the scenic panorama before them. Paul threw the bottle down the cliff as hard as he could; it shattered on the way down.

'If you want a drink, go and get it,' Marcos swiftly turned to Whisky with a sneer and gave him a push. Off-balance, Whisky hurtled down over rocks and sticks to lie in a crumpled heap at the bottom.

That's problem two. No more free grog or telling tales for that old sot, Paul smiled to himself, now for issue three. He climbed back into the Ute, a smug grin spreading across his dark features. A dust tail curled behind the Ute as Paul sped back the way he'd come until the turnoff. Following the new track, Paul slowed down, searching for a thicket of mulga and bullock bush. Making sure the Ute was well hidden in a dense patch of scrub, he sat smoking and contemplating his future. A yacht to entertain beautiful Greek women would be the first acquisition. He would introduce himself to Greek society as a respected businessman from Melbourne, Australia.

The roar of a vehicle brought Marcos out of his reverie. He peered from the bushes down the track towards the sound of the approaching car. Seeing it was Tom's Landrover, he left the scrub's shade and began walking along the road as though stranded.

Returning from his mine, Tom recognized the man in the middle of the road. I wonder what Marcos is doing out here on foot this time of the day. He must have broken down. Wonder where his Ute is? Can't see it anywhere.

'Have you broken down, Paul?' Tom leaned out of the window of his Land Rover, 'Want a ride back to town? Hop in, and I'll drive you back.'

Paul opened the driver's side door quickly and yanked Tom roughly from the vehicle. Tom, taken by surprise, found himself lying on the ground. Paul dealt him a kick in the stomach which had him curled into a foetal position, gagging. Another kick in the back had him on the verge of unconsciousness. Blows rained down on his defenceless head and shoulders, and Tom remembered no more. Marcos headed back to the township with all the speed he dared in Tom's vehicle but not before he'd checked to see what was in the back of the Land Rover. Satisfied the bags held raw opals, Paul detoured to his shed. Parking the vehicle inside out of sight of prying eyes, he unloaded the bags.

What a haul, I'll be rich forever, he thought; my dream villa on an Aegean isle has come true. The bags safely stowed in the shed; Marcos jumped in the Land Rover and drove off for the rest of the haul.

***

Tom couldn't tell how long he had been unconscious; he heard someone groan and then became aware that the sound was coming from his lips. He tried to move but fell into a vortex of darkness. Tom's mind cleared as consciousness took over. There could be some broken ribs and maybe other internal injuries because of the pain and nausea. The attack had happened so quickly that he was unable to defend himself. Tom's mind full of bewildering and conflicting thoughts, his body so full of pain that he couldn't think straight.

He dimly remembered meeting Paul Marcos. Maybe somebody attacked them both and dragged Marcos off? He could only remember Paul walking along the road and no one else. Indeed Paul wasn't his attacker? He was a helpful sort of bloke and respected by the community as a generous and useful man. So then who could have attacked him?

A vague thought of why he should be getting back to Dot worried him. When he was eventually able to lift his head, he couldn't see his vehicle. He blinked to clear his eyes, but the road was empty, and he lay back to gather strength and try to figure out once more who had attacked him and driven off in his Land Rover.

He surfaced again, his mind clear, the realization he was severely beaten established. He tried to roll over onto his stomach but fell back, swamped in pain and nausea. He could not figure out which part hurt the most.

Tom remembered Paul Marcos, who pulled him from the vehicle and attacked him and driven away with his opal. Thoughts of Dot flashed across his mind; oh, no! All that opal stored in the van, and she's there on her own.

How long had he been lying there? The sun had sunk low in the sky. If Paul had beaten him senseless, what would he not do to Dot? What sort of a man was Marcos if he could appear so upright in the community and then beat up unsuspecting folks like me. If he could beat me senseless, what would he do to Dot? Oh, God! He groaned. I have to try and save her somehow.

He rolled over onto his stomach, then tried to draw up his knees but was immediately sick. He lay on the ground until nausea passed. Blood and sweat trickled into his eyes, a jackhammer pounded inside his head; after a couple of attempts, he wavered drunkenly to his feet only to topple over again. The thought of what could be happening to Dot drove him to his knees, and he began to crawl along the track painfully.

Somewhere in the distance, an engine purred. Was it the attacker come to finish him off? Tom felt vulnerable and helpless. Maybe it was someone going home from his mine? He hoped it was not Marcos. Tom tried to get his bearings, but his mind refused to function. Maybe he was going away from town? A sob broke from his lips. Oh, Dot! I'm sorry I'm not there for you, and with a superhuman effort, he dragged himself a few more yards.

A voice broke through the cotton wool in his head,

'Struth!' Nicki punched the air angrily as he saw the plight of his erstwhile friend.

'Who's the rotter that did this to you, Tom?' Anger and guilt flooded through Nicki as he tried to wipe Tom's face with a piece of rag.

'Dot! She's in danger. Opal in the caravan…' Tom gasped.

'Don't worry, old mate. I'll get the Mine's Officer to check her out.' Nicki hurried to the Toyota and called Ian Flemming on the two-way radio, explaining what had happened.

'I'll get around to Dot's immediately.' Ian responded

Nicki gently stood Tom on his feet and half carried him to the vehicle pushing him into the passenger seat. He drove like a maniac along twisting tracks and between mullock heaps, dodging trees and stumps in a mad rush to get Tom to the Health clinic and help.

'Dot… Help Dot…!' Tom urged between bouts of fainting and nausea.

'Ian Flemming is on his way, mate; he'll take care of her. We've got to get help for you. You certainly got the worst end of someone's boot. Do you know who it was?'

'Yeah, but you …wo - won't … believe me.' Tom muttered.

'Try me,' Nicki replied tersely.

'Paul Marcos!'

'You've got to be joking! Paul wouldn't do a thing like this. He's too decent a fellow.' Surprise made Nicki swerve suddenly, and Tom let out a yell of pain.

'Do you have to drive like a bull at a gate? And I'm not kidding.' Tom insisted, trying to sit forward to make his point; the movement sent him spinning into unconsciousness. 'It was Marcos!' his voice drifted away along with his senses.

***

Ian Flemming was just about to leave his office and take a look around the township, checking to see if all was quiet when the radio crackled into life. Nicki Callis's voice came over the air reporting that he had found Tom near dead and that Dot was in danger.

'Will do that, Nicki. I'm on my way.' Ian hung up the receiver and hurried out to his 4 WD station wagon that had been modified into a police van and headed for the caravan park. Ian had full authority to administer law and order in Mintabie and the tribal lands in the absence of any police presence. He took the policing side of his job very seriously.

As he approached, the boom of a shotgun echoed through the caravan park. Cold fingers of dread curled around Ian's heart at what he would find. Amid clouds of dust, Ian ran into the lean-to.

Dot was lying on the floor gagging. She had been punched in the stomach and about the head. A masked figure was standing over her, holding a shotgun to her head with one hand and holding his blood-soaked shoulder with the other. The intruder looked up in surprise as Ian burst into the room. Marcos had not heard the Police van arrive. The dratted woman was putting up a fight.

'Put the gun down, or I'll blow your brains out.' Ian barked; his gun aimed steadily at the intruder's head. Rage coursed through Ian as he glimpsed Dot lying on the floor. She could be dead. The intruder slowly laid the gun down near his feet, all the time watching Ian closely.

'Take off that scarf, and let's get a good look at the coward who can beat up a woman and steal her opal.' Ian ground out the order.

The intruder hesitated, but Ian waved the gun threateningly and moved in, pulling the scarf away from the intruder's face.

'Paul Marcos! What are you doing here?' Ian gawked at the Greek. He had worked tirelessly to get a health clinic and school established. He had done so much good for the town. What had caused him to become a thief and maybe a murderer? Must he have earned enough money out of the supermarket?

Paul was not slow to take advantage of Ian's surprise and landed a punch in Ian's stomach; he folded up, dropping to the floor.

Dot saw her opportunity and aimed a kick at Marcos's shins. He let out a howl, dancing around, clutching his leg.

'That's for Benjie,' Dot screamed her anger, pain and fear.

Marcos turned on Dot, aiming a kick at her head. Ian had regained enough breath to charge the man knocking him down, falling on top of him and holding him down until the handcuffs were on.

'OK, Paul! What's this all about?' Ian gasped, sitting on top of his prisoner, trying to catch his breath.

'She's a madwoman. She shot me,' the Greek defended, belligerently, trying to get up.

'What were you doing to make her shoot at you?' Ian looked around the blood-splattered room and the motionless form of Benjie.

Dot had risen and staggered to a chair.

'I wanted to buy their opal, but she shot me.' Marcos felt he could manipulate Ian.

'Funny, but I don't believe you, Paul. You're coming with me. We'll pay a visit to the Police Station at Marla Bore. You can tell them your story.'

'I want a lawyer and a doctor.' Paul protested, refusing to look Ian in the eye. 'I'm bleeding to death. If I die, you'll be up for murder.'

'You'll get a lawyer, don't worry.' Ian assured him, securing his prisoner to the caravan. He then phoned the Health Clinic to see if the nurse could come and get Dot.

'I can't leave the clinic. I'm attending Tom Marsden. Nicki Callas has just brought him in. Tom's been beaten senseless.'

'OK. Tell Nicki to get around here fast. Dot needs attention. She's taken a beating as well.'

'Has someone gone mad in the town?' The nurse wanted to know.

'Paul Marcos!' Ian was terse.

'What! Paul Marcos?' the nurse repeated in shock. 'What's he done? He's Mintabie's unofficial mayor.'

'I'll explain later. I'm taking Marcos to Marla to charge him with murder.' Ian drove the sixty kilometres to Marla Bore, his prisoner safely secured. Ian's mind began to run back over the past couple of years, piecing together many events. There were spates of break-ins and opal thefts from time to time, but he didn't make any arrests due to a lack of evidence. Yarns of claim jumping, fights, and thievery did the round of the outback community, causing a lot of anxiety. Still, when he tried to pin down where the rumours were coming from, he could not find where the stories began or evidence that anything was wrong. People seemed to clam up, and there were no reports of suspicious behaviour.

The Aborigines caught the blame, but they were probably used as scapegoats to hide the real culprits; Ian could see that now. But he was not willing to accuse the Aboriginal people of any involvement in this latest attack, nor could he quite equate Paul Marcos with any wrongdoing. The evidence, however, was stacking up against the Greek.

Funnily enough, Marcos always knew who had discovered opal and who had suffered theft. He was first on the scene shouting for Ian to do something and threatening to have him moved elsewhere because he was inept as a peace officer. Marcos always aired his views loudly, and everyone agreed with him. It was the case of the loudest voice heard and believed. If the Greek knew what had happened, had he orchestrated the crime? Because of the unsolved crimes, the community was always in a state of nervous excitement and unrest. What had happened to the Marsden's showed that something was going on behind the scene. He resolved to investigate each incident.

Ian's thought's turned in another direction; where was the Korean who supposedly found opal and then hot-footed it back to Korea? People left the minefield; no one heard of them nor thought to make enquiries about them, least of all he. He'd just assumed the Korean had returned to his home country. At the first opportunity, he would look into the matter.

The Police Sergeant at Marla Bore greeted Ian with a great deal of scepticism,

'I hope you've got evidence to prove your accusations against Mr Marcos.'

Ian knew that he didn't have at this stage, but he had to crack Marcos somehow. 'Were you going to throw the Marsden's down a mineshaft just like you did the Korean?' It was a long shot, and Ian hoped it would pay off. Marcos blanched and sat a bit straighter in his chair. Bingo! I've hit the jackpot, Ian exalted inwardly.

'What are you talking about?' the would-be mayor hedged.

Ian turned to the Sergeant, 'Will you come back to Mintabie with me. And we'll search a certain mineshaft that I remember Paul here once saying was the perfect spot to dispose of a body?'

The Sergeant cleared his throat doubtfully, 'I'm swamped at this moment. There is 'Men's Business' being held out at Indulkana. There is a lot of fear generated at these events, and I figure I hadn't better be away. Tell you what, you go and take a look. Get somebody to go with you.'

'On condition that you do not let my prisoner go until you hear from me.' Ian bargained.

'You won't find anything there,' sneered the Greek, but he was uncomfortable. 'I've done nothing wrong, and you can't keep me here. Where is my lawyer?'

'You have been charged with a serious crime of assault and break-in, so you can stay in a cell overnight. We can't get a lawyer until tomorrow afternoon,' the Sergeant was embarrassed at having to keep Paul Marcos, philanthropist, in prison overnight, but he was over a barrel. He turned, pinning Ian with fierce blue eyes, his moustache bristling with the threat, 'If you don't find evidence that this man has committed a crime by 9 am tomorrow, he's walking free.'

Ian grinned, saluted the Sergeant and disappeared.

Driving through Mintabie, Ian saw Nicki Callas standing outside of the Health Clinic and stopped.

'How is the Marsden's?' he called out.

'Tom has a couple of broken ribs and a concussion. His kidney damaged. Won't know until the X-rays are available. The Flying Doctor is coming for him first thing tomorrow. Dorothy is OK, just severe bruising. She'll go to Alice with Tom for a check-up.'

Nicki approached Ian, leaning through the driver's side window, 'Sure you haven't made a mistake, Flemming, arresting Paul.' He could not get his head around the fact that Paul had beaten Tom so cruelly and threatened Dot's life with the intent to steal their opal.

'Why don't you come with me, Nicki? I'm going to investigate a certain mineshaft and its contents. First, I must pick up a rope and tackle and a ladder. I'm going to get Joe Palmer from the hardware store to come along. I want you guys as witnesses.'

'What for?' Nicki asked as he climbed into the passenger seat

'I'll explain on the way.' Ian let in the clutch and took off for the Hardware store.

On the way, the two men again voiced their concern that Ian had wrongly accused Paul Marcos even though the evidence showed he was present when the Marsden's were attacked. Joe thought Ian was out of his mind at the old disused mineshaft, 'What do you expect to find out here.' He was edgy, remembering how Marcos had helped him out not long ago when his mine proved to be dry, and he had no money for food or shoes for his kids.

'I want you blokes to lower me down this shaft. I believe I will have enough evidence to incriminate Marcos. But Ian was not prepared for what he would find at the bottom of the shaft.

In silence, the two men anchored the rope to the vehicle, and Ian tied himself to the other end. He clamped a hard hat on his head with a miner's light on it and began the descent. There were feelings of trepidation in Ian as the two men lowered him down the shaft. What if they decided to drop him down there and leave? It was clear they doubted that Marcos had committed any wrong even though Nicki saw how bad the attack on the Marsden's was and the evidence pointing to Paul being the perpetrator.

The shaft was maybe 30 feet deep, and as Ian dropped down, he could see in the light from his hat an enormous pile of rubbish on the bottom. When he was closer, he realized the garbage was a pile of bodies in different decomposition stages. On the top was the shape of an Aboriginal and then the shrivelled form that could have been the Korean. Bile rose in Ian's throat, and his stomach wanted to empty itself. He jerked the rope, informing the men above to pull him up. He couldn't stand being in that terrible place any longer.

Ian moved across to his police wagon and sat in the driver's seat, his head bowed. He ran his fingers through his hair in agitation.

'What's wrong?' Joe and Nicki spoke together.

'You look like you've seen a ghost.' Nicki said.

'You don't want to know.' Ian felt he'd been run over by a bulldozer as the enormity of his find hit home. He reached for his two-way radio and called the police at Marla and explained what he had found.

'You blokes roll out this tape and secure the crime scene. I'll go back to the office and wait for the police to arrive. Ian glanced at the two anxious men. He realized he owed them an explanation. Besides, he'd explode if he didn't debrief of the horror unearthed.

'It's graveyard down there. There must be half a dozen bodies dumped in that shaft. All those people who were supposed to have gone home to their families or left the country are down there, and I'll bet their fortunes are in Marcos's bank account in Greece.' Anger, betrayal and shame at being so quickly taken in by a glib tongue threatened to swamp Ian. He was going to make sure the Greek had the book thrown at him.

It was dark by the time the police arrived, but they had generators and lights, and at the mine site, everything as bright as day. The bodies and remains of bodies rose to the surface. All human remains identified in Adelaide owing to lack of facilities in the outback. There was enough evidence here to see that Paul Marcos would be put away for a very long time.

It was into the new day by the time Ian returned to his caravan. But the horror was still with him. He could not rid his mind of the grizzly scene down the mineshaft. He was not a drinking man, but he reached for a bottle of brandy to help him forget for a while.

Battling a sore head the next day, Ian called on Dot and Tom at the clinic before the Flying Doctor whisked them off to Alice Springs.

Dot was in a blue dressing gown, sitting by Tom's bed, holding his hand in her good one. A livid bruise showed down her left cheek, and her eyes were mere slits. Her lips swollen so that it was hard for her to talk. Her other hand was bandaged to a board, indicating fingers had been stomped on and broken. Tom's face rearranged into a caricature of its former contours. Propped up, bandages around his head and chest, Tom tried to crack hardy. At the sight of Ian, Tom rasped,

'Thanks for saving Dot, Ian. I don't know what I would have done if anything had happened to her.'

'I've got to get a statement from you both about yesterday's events,' Ian's face was grim and his voice rough with anger. Are you able to tell us what happened, Dot?'

Tears seeped through the slits of Dot's swollen eyes as she nodded assent and began to relate the events as they unfolded.

'After Tom left to go out to our mine, I had an awful forewarning that all was not right and glanced out of the window. Somebody was hiding in the bushes staring at our van, I could just see the outline, and I thought he could have been an Aboriginal. I was terrified and was just going to call Tom on the radio when I saw Paul Marcos get out and chase the man. They ran off over the creek into the bush, and I never saw them again. I tried to call up Tom, but he must have been away from the Land Rover and didn't hear my call.

When I looked out again, the Ute had disappeared. Everything went quiet until a bit later, I heard our Land Rover pull up. I would go to the door and open it to let Tom in, but Benjie was going bonkers, and I tried to quiet him.

'I couldn't,' Tom broke in. 'I was lying on the road, half-dead.'

Dot fell silent, her eyes fixed on the far wall of the clinic, and suddenly dismayed by how close they had both come to death.

'And then?' prompted Ian, bringing her back to the present.

'Benjie was still going mad, and then I knew a stranger was out there.'

'Dot, let me in.' the voice sounded familiar, but I couldn't quite put a name to it.

'Who is it?' I had to yell; Benjie was making such a racket.

'It's Nicki Callas.'

Not likely! He isn't our friend anymore; I knew the situation was dangerous. Someone out there was intent on obtaining our hard-earned opal, but who?

I tried to calm the fear that knotted my stomach and steady my hands. I grabbed the gun and waited. I wondered if I could aim accurately; I was shaking like a jelly. If only Tom were here! I wished. The door rattled, and the voice spoke again.

'Dot, let me in. Tom asked me to give you a message.'

That was nearly my undoing; what's the matter with Tom that he has to send a message through someone? Why didn't he call me on the two-way? I wondered what to do next. Quietly I lifted the receiver again, but I could only hear static. Where was Tom? I had never felt so alone in my life. I thought about giving him the opal, but I remembered how hard we had worked and what the gems would mean to our retirement. I got angry; what kind of man is he to prey on helpless people and take what they worked hard to amass. I said to myself; you'll have to take our opal over my dead body.

Footsteps crunched around the caravan stopping at each window, testing to see if an entry could be found, finally stopping at the larger window of the lean-to.'

'Come on, you old cow! Open up! Your old man's met his death. I've done for him. I'm coming for the opal. There was no pretext now of being Nicki Callas. The window smashed, spraying glass everywhere. A figure attempted to climb through, but Benjie attacked. The form flung Benjie against the wall. He yelped piteously, hurt dreadfully. It was a senseless act and made me see red.

Benjie tried to attack again, but the intruder flung him against the wall, and he just lay still. 'My brave little warrior.' Dot's voice quivered to a stop, and tears coursed down her swollen cheeks; she caught her lips between her teeth to keep from breaking down.

I aimed the gun at the figure standing just inside the window, but I couldn't point because I thought it looked a bit like Paul Marcos. I was so surprised I'd heard he was a good man.

Paul was laughing, 'you couldn't hit a fly. I'm not scared of you, you sill old cow. Show me where the opal is.'

'O-o-over my dead body,' I stuttered, aiming again as he started to come at me, 'It will be over your dead body, old girl,' he jeered. There was an explosion of sound, and smoke seemed to fill the room. I had hit Paul in the shoulder. The impact drove him back against the wall, but before I could gather my senses, Paul dived at me and punched me in the face. I fell; he kicked the gun from my hand, demanding, 'Where's the opal? Tell me, or I'll kill you.'

I couldn't think straight. Paul then started to pull everything apart, searching for the opal. My head cleared, and I reached for the gun. Paul caught my movement.

'Oh no, you don't!' he stamped on my fingers, picked up the gun, held it to my head.

I thought, this is it; I'm dead! I waited to follow Tom and Benjie.

Then I heard, 'Put down the gun, or I'll blow your brains out.' It was you, Ian. You'd entered the room. We were so intent on each other we didn't see or hear you come in. Well, you know the rest.'

'Yes, I remember. I had to take a risk to shoot Marcos before he shot you. He would have liked to shoot us both if he thought he could've got away with it. Even to the last, he's claimed innocence.'

'Instead, Paul gave me a kick in the ribs.' Dot flinched as pain shot through her chest.

Ian looked at the couple, he was trying to hide a tear, and these two were incredibly brave. Because of them, I've uncovered a series of dreadful crimes committed by someone who dares call himself a pillar of society. He almost got away with murder.

The door opened, and Nicki and Maria Callas stood there. Maria rushed to Dot's side, clasping her in her arms, 'Oh Dot, how are you? I thought you were going to die yesterday when I saw you. I'm so sorry for the way I have behaved. I should have known better and been there for you.'

Dot laid her head on Maria's shoulder and sobbed, 'I was so scared. I thought Tom was already dead. He killed Benjie and would have killed me.'

Nicki grabbed Tom's hand and squeezed it gently, 'Sorry, old mate. Don't know what got into us? It was all that talk about you doing Whisky out of his claim and taking opal that belonged to him. We were ready to lynch you.'

Ian's interest sparked again, 'what's this about Whisky having a claim? I haven't registered any claims in his name. What's more, he's never done a day's work in his life.'

'Paul told everyone at the pub that Tom had stolen Whisky's claim. He claimed to be Whisky's carer and was going to get the opal back for him.' Nicki explained. 'He said Tom was a crook and should go to gaol. By the way, we found the old drunk at the bottom of the cliff near Clement's camp. He's OK. He's so pickled with booze he didn't even get a broken bone in the fall.'

'How did Whisky end up at the bottom of the cliff? Have I missed something? Where is Whisky now? I need to talk to him.' Ian realized again how Marcos manipulated the community behind his back. 'Why wasn't I informed of Whisky's fall?'

'Whisky's in the pub now; he's the toast of the town. Everyone is buying him a drink. You might have to let him sleep it off before you talk to him.' Nicki grinned.

'I think I'd better try and get Whisky to give me a statement. Besides, I have to find out who the Aboriginal is.

'The yarn going around is the Aboriginal is Billy Quattro. He was boasting a couple of nights ago how easy it would be to get the white man's opal. No-one has seen him around.' Nicki offered the tit-bit of information to bring Ian up to date with what was happening in the town. Ian lived in the settlement but didn't know any of what Nicki was telling him.

'Why wasn't I told any of this?' Ian was angry, blaming himself for not listening carefully to the rumours.

'Marcos used to say you were hopeless and wouldn't listen. He was always running you down. Anyway, we all thought that's all they were, stories.' Nike's glance at Ian was accusing.

'To think we listened to the yarns and believed them,' shame flushed Maria's cheeks, 'we should have known better. But the stories did seem to make sense.'

'The trouble is, here in Mintabie, nobody trusts anyone else,' Nicki rubbed his hands over his face. 'We're all afraid of being robbed and killed, and so we keep everything to ourselves.'

'Well, Paul Marcos won't be spreading any more rumours again. He's in the lock-up at Marla Bore. He'll be put away for a very long time for murder.' Ian predicted, just shows how easy it is to manipulate a small isolated group of people like Mintabie with innuendo, lies and fear. Ian looked at Nicki and Maria, but they avoided eye contact with him.

'What will you two do when you are better? Finish your holiday?' Still overcome by how badly she had behaved toward Dot, Maria hoped for a second chance at being a friend to Dot.

'Over my dead body!' Dot was emphatic. 'We're going back to Melbourne and safe old suburbia.'

ABOUT THE AUTHOR

My writing life is like a rainbow cake – layer upon layer.
The first layer was compiling the church news-letter. It was illustrated, and newsy.
No church news-letter was ever like it.

Then came the journalistic layer. Great heights were reached with an article in the Women's Weekly and working as a journalist for the local newspaper, The Transcontinental. There were farming and gardening magazines included in that layer.

The biography layer came next. Three biographies were self-published. Several other short biographies written. It is so interesting and necessary to record people's stories for history's sake.

Like cream between the layers I practised the art of short story writing.

The present layer is blogging. I have a blog site and it covers my writing life from short stories, journalistic articles, photography, and anything that demands to be written and read.

I love this writing life.

www.ingramcontent.com/pod-product-compliance
Lightning Source LLC
Chambersburg PA
CBHW011148290426
44109CB00023B/2528